The Scots-Irish in Pennsylvania and Kentucky

Best wishes
to Helen
Billy Kennedy

by
BILLY KENNEDY

The Scots-Irish in Pennsylvania and Kentucky
© 1998 Billy Kennedy

First published September, 1998

THE SCOTS-IRISH CHRONICLES

Scots-Irish in the Hills of Tennessee (published 1995)
Scots-Irish in the Shenandoah Valley (published 1996)
Scots-Irish in the Carolinas (published 1997)
Scots-Irish in Pennsylvania and Kentucky (published 1998)

PRINTED IN NORTHERN IRELAND

Published by

Causeway Press

Ambassador Publications
a division of
Ambassador Productions Ltd.
Providence House
Ardenlee Street, Belfast, BT6 8QJ Northern Ireland
www.ambassador-productions.com

Emerald House
427 Wade Hampton Blvd.
Greenville SC 29609, USA
www.emeraldhouse.com

About *the Author*

BILLY KENNEDY has written three other books on the Scots-Irish, all of them best-sellers on both sides of the Atlantic. He carried out considerable research in Northern Ireland and in the United States to authenticate 'The Scots-Irish in the Hills of Tennessee' (published 1995), 'The Scots-Irish in the Shenandoah Valley' (published 1996) and 'The Scots-Irish in the Carolinas' (published 1997). Preparatory work for this fourth book, 'The Scots-Irish in Pennsylvania and Kentucky', was just as extensive. Billy Kennedy, born in Belfast in 1943 and a resident of Co Armagh for most of his life, comes from an Ulster-Scots Presbyterian background. He is a journalist of wide recognition in Northern Ireland over a period of more than 25 years. With the Ulster/Belfast News Letter, a newspaper which was founded in 1737, he has been a news editor for 18 years and assistant editor and leader writer for five. He now operates as a full-time freelance journalist, public relations consultant and author, combining regular column work for the News Letter on a wide range of subjects and news coverage for other press and media outlets in Northern Ireland. His abiding interest is concentrated in the history of the Scots-Irish settlements on the American frontier. Through his authorship, Billy Kennedy has lectured on the Scots-Irish diaspora in America in major cities and towns in the south eastern Appalachian region. He is an authority on American country music and culture, travels to Nashville regularly and he has interviewed for the Ulster/Belfast News Letter singing stars such as Willie Nelson, Garth Brooks, Charley Pride, George Jones, Reba McEntire, Kenny Rogers, George Hamilton IV, Billy Walker, Ricky Skaggs and Crystal Gayle. Billy Kennedy is also a specialist on sport and religious affairs, and for 30 years he has written and compiled various publications for soccer internationally and on the local domestic football scene in Northern Ireland. He has been a director of Linfield Football Club, Ireland's leading soccer club, for 25 years. He has also compiled and edited books on cultural traditions in Ireland, including two on the history of the Orange Order. He is married with a grown-up daughter.

Dedication

*This book is dedicated to my loving wife Sally,
daughter Julie and my parents.*

*"The wise in heart will be called a discerning man, and
pleasant speech will increase learning."
– Proverbs, chapter 16, verse 21.*

*The author acknowledges the help and support given to him in the
compilation of this book by Samuel Lowry, of Ambassador
Productions, Gregory Campbell of Causeway Press and Tomm
Knutson, of Emerald House. It was again a team effort!*

List *of contents*

Cover Illustrations

The movement of frontiersman Daniel Boone and the Scots-Irish pioneers along the Wilderness Road through the Cumberland Gap into Kentucky. (Painting by Claude Regnier after the painting by George Caleb Bingham). Published by agreement with and courtesy of the Missouri Historical Society, St Louis. George Caleb Bingham was a politician and artist of Scots-Irish roots, born at Franklin, Missouri in 1811. He was a member of the Missouri legislature and served as state treasurer in 1862-65 and adjutant general of Missouri in 1875. Bingham was an artist with a talent for skilfully packing his canvasses with characters and action. In later life he became more absorbed with landscapes, concentrating on light and space. The last years of his life were spent teaching at the University of Missouri.

Inset pictures: President James Buchanan. The Great Seal of America designed by Ulster-born 18th American statesman Charles Thomson, who was secretary to the US Continental Congress.

Thanks

In compiling this book I would gratefully acknowledge the tremendous help and assistance given to me by so many people in the United States. Right across the Appalachian states and from other American regions, I have received a great reservoir of information on the Scots-Irish families who moved to the frontier during the 18th century. I sincerely appreciate the time and effort taken by those to whom the Scots-Irish tradition and culture means so much and I greatly value the many letters of support sent to me for this project. I trust that through this book, and my previous works "The Scots-Irish in the Hills of Tennessee", "The Scots-Irish in the Shenandoah Valley" and "The Scots-Irish in the Carolinas", many people will come to know and understand better the sacrifices made by a strong resolute people in creating a civilisation and a structured way of life in a wilderness. The United States would not be the great nation that it is today had it not been for the pioneering spirit of the Scots-Irish Presbyterian settlers of the 18th century. Their valour and outstanding achievements make them a special people.

BILLY KENNEDY

The author can be contacted at:
49, Knockview Drive,
Tandragee,
Craigavon,
Northern Ireland BT62 2BH.

Foreword *from the United States*

Dr. John Rice Irwin

Since the early days of our history, men have written of their ties with the old country - tracing their ancestry, or the ancestors of the people about whom they wrote, to England, Ireland, Scotland, Wales, Germany, France or to other foreign countries. On the other hand, the people from these old countries have understandably expressed less interest in what happened to the brothers and kin of their ancestors who came to America.

My beloved friend the late Alex Haley discussed this subject one spring morning as we drove up Tennessee's beautiful Powell Valley and into Middlesboro, Kentucky. The names on mail boxes and on the hand-lettered signs at country stores, fix-it-shops and service stations, promoted Alex to ask the question: "You know," he said, "I've often wondered if the kinsfolks of the emigrants who left those countries and came to America - I wonder if they wondered and were curious as to what happened to the brothers and sisters of their great, great grandparents who left their little cottages and came to the new world never to be heard of again?"

I do not know the extent to which the talk around the family hearthstone of the families of Northern Europe turned to the old folks who left for the new world so long ago. But we do know that one man, a born and bred Scots-Irish man from Northern Ireland did wonder.

His name is Billy Kennedy and his first foray into the study of the subject resulted in the book, The Scots-Irish in the Hills of Tennessee. The work was well received, and he rushed headlong into a second volume, The Scots-Irish in the Shenandoah Valley, soon followed by The Scots-Irish in the Carolinas.

Now he comes forward with his fourth book: The Scots-Irish in Pennsylvania and Kentucky. This work, like the other three volumes, not only details the interesting and important contributions made by his kin to the American society, but it bespeaks the pride he has of his people, revealed on every page, and justly so.

Maybe no such tiny a peace of land in the world has had more influence on American history and culture than of the province of Ulster in Northern Ireland.

Just as the other books by Billy Kennedy have done, this one will likely titillate local and regional historians to study and research their own history with renewed interest and enthusiasm. If, for example, Bill Monroe is of interest in Londonderry, Northern Ireland, then perhaps the people in Rosine, Kentucky will be more inclined to take notice of the "Father of Bluegrass Music" and to observe him in a more substantive, studious and appreciative manner.

The same can be said for the hundreds of other historic people, places and events from Pennsylvania and Kentucky with Scots-Irish connections herein chronicled. The book will hopefully serve as a catalyst to "get people to talking", thinking and to raising questions, and eventually to studying, not only their Scots-Irish connections, but their total history, culture and heritage.

DR JOHN RICE IRWIN
Museum of Appalachia, Norris, Tennessee.

* DR JOHN RICE IRWIN is founder and director of the Museum of Appalachia in Norris, Tennessee, a farm-village settlement which has gained publicity and acclaim throughout the United States, and beyond. He is a former college, university and public school teacher and has served as both school principal and country school superintendent. He has also engaged successfully in farming, real estate, Appalachian music (he has his own eight-member string band), and several small businesses and corporations which he started.

Dr Irwin's main interest, however, lies in the people of his native Southern Appalachian Mountains. Since childhood he has spent virtually all his spare time visiting and talking with these mountain folk which he admires and loves. He is considered to be one of the leading authorities on the history, culture and people of Southern Appalachia, and on the American pioneer-frontier life in general. John Rice Irwin, born of pioneer ancestors of a Scots-Irish and Welsh lineage, is a prolific author, having written five books on life in the Southern Appalachian region.

The books are listed:
• Musical Instruments of the Southern Appalachian Mountains - 1979
• Guns and Gunmaking, Tools of Southern Appalachia - 1980
• Baskets and Basket Making in Southern Appalachia - 1982
• A People and their Quilts - 1983
• Alex Stewart, Portrait of a Pioneer - 1985

"

They brought to America no submissive love for England; and their experience and their religion alike bade them meet opposition with prompt resistance. The first voice publicly raised in America to dissolve all connection with Great Britain came not from the Puritans of New England, or the Dutch of New York, or the planters of Virginia, but the Scotch-Irish Presbyterians.
A paradoxical fact regarding the Scotch-Irish is that they are very little Scotch and much less Irish. They do not belong mainly to the so-called Celtic race, but they are the most composite of all the people of the British Isles. They are called Scots because they lived in Scotia; and they are called Irish because they moved to Ireland. Geography and not ethnology has given them their name.

"

19th century American historian
GEORGE BANCROFT

"

Wherever the Scotch-Irish settled in America they started schools. As the parsons were the best educated men they taught the youth as part of their ministry. In time, the schools they started in their frontier congregations grew to be common schools for all. Later some of them became academies and a few became colleges and universities. In this way these Ulster Presbyterians did more to start schools in the South and West than any other people.

"

19th century American historian
CHARLES WILLIAM DABNEY

Foreword *from Northern Ireland*

Alister J. McReynolds

Within the province of Ulster the last five years have been a burgeoning interest in Lannans, the lowland Scots language, and in Ulster Scots/Appalachian history. I'm sure this is due in no small part to Billy Kennedy's journalistic observations of the Scots-Irish contribution to the historical development of Tennessee, Virginia and the Carolinas.

This new book links two states which are not often joined in the popular imagination - Pennsylvania and Kentucky. True, Ulster-Scots had brilliant battle campaigns in the Civil War - General Alexander M. McCook of the Union Army at Perryville, Kentucky and General Lafayette McLaws of the Confederates at Gettysburg in Pennsylvania. But such was the scale of the Ulster-Scots contribution that the same could be said of almost any two states. No - the answer runs deeper and has to do with the mechanism inside which the pioneering and foundation takes place.

In the case of Pennsylvania when William Penn asked fellow Quaker James Logan from Lurgan, Co. Armagh to help him form a colony in 1699 he already knew that Ulstermen made good soldiers. After all, Penn had seen military service in Carrickfergus in 1666 in the days before pacifism overcame him

Even though relationships between Ulstermen and Quakers in Pennsylvania were not good the latter saw the value in establishing Ulster settlers to their immediate west as a buffer against marauding Indians. Inside this buffer zone, Quaker radicalism and democracy could then flourish. So by 1730 the interior of the state contained townships with names such as Derry, Donegal, Tyrone and Coleraine.

In the case of Kentucky we see this Quaker/Ulster-Scots combination again. When in 1769 Daniel Boone, who was of Quaker origin, set out to carve the state of Kentucky from the wilderness he took with him men with names such as Harland and MacBride and these were quickly followed by other Ulster-Scots such as James and Robert McAfee and Simon Butler.

Once again Billy Kennedy makes fulsome comment on the development of American country and folk music and the enormous contribution of people like Bill Monroe. In no other state does this music fulfil so well the description of being "white man's blues" as it does in the coalmining region of Kentucky. I well recall a television interview given some years ago by Phil Everly and his brother Don from Brownie in Meelenboro county, Kentucky when they commented on how disappointed they were that they could not find anyone called Everly in Ireland.

I would respectfully suggest that they might start looking amongst the Averley families of Armagh and Down. In early Appalachia spellings and pronunciations didn't always remain constant.

Inside Pennsylvania enormous inputs to civilisation were made by Quaker radicals such as John Woolam, who contributed mightily to the ending of the slave trade. But arguably it was the Ulstermen who carried the instinct for holding borderlands who created the conditions which allowed democratic ideas to flourish and created a safe haven that attracted other European pietists such as the Amish who moved in and eventually displaced the Quakers.

Billy Kennedy's latest publication certainly tells the stories of these border people with vigour and colour.

ALISTER J. McREYNOLDS, MA, BEd, DASE, DLIS, FRSA,
Principal and Director Lisburn Institute of Further and
Higher Education, Co Antrim.
July 1998.

* ALISTER JOHN McREYNOLDS, who has strong family links with Ulster-Scots settlers who pioneered the American frontier in the 18th century, is a chartered librarian as well as being a qualified teacher. Educated at Stranmillis College (Belfast), Queen's University (Belfast) and the University of Ulster, he is a fellow of the Royal Society of Arts with an interest in local history. He is chairman of the Lisburn Historical Society and a director of the Ulster/New Zealand Trust.

The McReynolds clan first moved to America in 1737 from the homeland in Killyman, Co. Tyrone and members of the family settled first in Maryland and Pennsylvania, and then in Virginia and Tennessee. Two descendants of the pioneering McReynolds of the mid-18th century were prominent US politicians and statesmen in the early part of this century: James Clark McReynolds, who was attorney general in the administration of President Woodrow Wilson, and Samuel Davis McReynolds, leader of the US House of Representatives Foreign Affairs Committee during the Presidential term of Franklin D. Roosevelt.

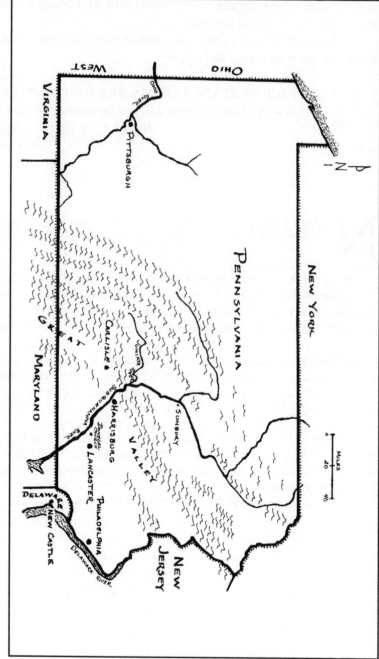

Pennsylvania

1

Northern *Ireland*

Northern Ireland is an integral part of the United Kingdom with a population of 1.6 million.The geographical boundary takes in six of the nine counties of the province of Ulster. The majority of the population, almost two-thirds, are Protestant and British by culture and tradition, and committed to maintaining the constitutional link with the United Kingdom.

Just over one-third of the population is Roman Catholic, most of whom are Irish by culture and tradition and seek the reunification of Ireland through a constitutional link-up with the Republic of Ireland. A sizeable number of Roman Catholics in Northern Ireland favour the status quo link with Britain, therefore the political break-down cannot be taken on a sectarian headcount.

The one million Protestants in Northern Ireland are descendants of Scottish and English settlers who moved from the British mainland in the 17th and 18th centuries. Presbyterians, who formed the bulk of those emigrating to the American frontier lands in the 18th century, are today the most numerous Protestant tradition in Northern Ireland, totalling 400,000.The Church of Ireland (Anglican Episcopal) community accounts for 350,000 people, Methodists 70,000, with the smaller Protestant denominations accounting for the rest. Belfast (population 500,000), a city twinned with Nashville in Tennessee, is the capital of Northern Ireland and the six counties are Antrim, Down, Londonderry, Tyrone, Armagh and Fermanagh.

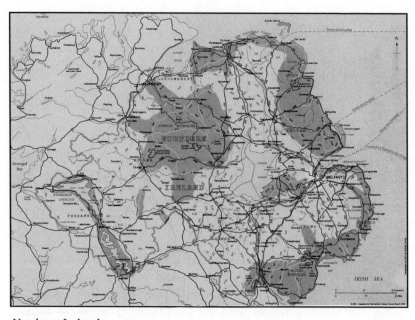

Northern Ireland

2

Pennsylvania - *the Keystone State*

Pennsylvania is one of America's oldest colonial territories, a state named after English Quaker colonialist Admiral William Penn in the late 17th century. Then, it was part of the American frontier for the white European settlers who crossed the Atlantic in simple wooden ships to start a fresh life in what they perceived as "the New World".

Today, Pennsylvania, a state running to 46,000 square miles and with 67 counties, has a population of just over twelve million, with its two main cities - Philadelphia and Pittsburgh - huge centres with diverse cultural assets, deep ethnic roots and strong civic pride. The Scots-Irish Presbyterian settlers of the 18th century were in at the early development of both cities and there is still a strong identity with this diaspora in the regions.

The capital of what is often described as the Keystone State is Harrisburg, an Eastern Pennsylvanian city also with strong Ulster-Scots roots, and the state motto is virtue, liberty and independence. Indeed, these ideals were obviously in the forefront of those who met at Independence Hall in Philadelphia on July 4, 1776 to sign the Declaration of Independence and to draw up the nation's constitution. Eight of the 56 signatories of the Declaration were of Scots-Irish descent.

The first Continental Congress of the United States gathered in this "city of brotherly love" in 1774 and Congress met there during most of the Revolutionary War. The Liberty Bell is one of the historical treasures in Philadelphia. Agriculture and tourism are Pennsylvania's largest industries and in 1995 United States and international travellers spent 20.5 billion dollars in the region. There are 50 natural lakes in Pennsylvania, over 20 acres wide, and rivers and streams run for 45,000 miles. There are 116 state forests.

The *United States*

The United States of America is made up of 50 states, each of which has its own government. The national government is based in the capital, Washington DC. The population of the USA is 257,800,000.

The country is dominated by two mountain ranges - the Rockies in the west and the Appalachians in the east. In between lie the flat, fertile Great Plains, which are used for farming. The United States is rich in natural resources. It has large deposits of raw materials such as iron, coal and oil, which are needed to produce industrial goods. These resources have helped the country to become the world's greatest industrial manufacturer. The United States is also rich in farmland, and exports large amounts of agricultural produce, especially cereals, cotton and tobacco. Most years, the United States exports more grain than all the other countries of the world combined.

The United States is often described as a "melting pot" because its population is a mix of many peoples. The country's first inhabitants were the American Indians. Later, settlers came from all over Europe, especially the British Isles, Germany, Scandinavia, France, Italy, Ireland and Poland. The United States black population are the descendants of slaves who were brought to America from Africa. More recent arrivals include Hispanics (Spanish-speakers) from Mexico and South America, and Asians.

3

Kentucky - *the Bluegrass State*

Kentucky has a motto very often used by the pro-Union population in Northern Ireland - United We Stand, Divided We Fall
- and it is a state with strong historical ties to Ulster, from the
first pioneer settlers who first entered the region with the legendary
American frontier explorer Daniel Boone in 1773.

The state, admitted to the Union on June 1, 1792, takes its name
from the Wyandot Indian word "Kem-tah-teh" (the land of tomorrow)
and it has also been referred to as the Bluegrass state, the Tobacco
state, the Hemp state, the Corncracker state, and that Dark and Bloody
Ground. The latter appellation was taken from the period of the late
18th century when the white settlers came into bitter and bloody conflict with the Indian tribes over the occupation of lands.

Over many years, Indian massacres and revenge killings by white
settlers stained the soil of this largely mountainous and wooded state
and it was well into the 19th century before hostilities ceased.

Today, Kentucky has a population of three and a half million, with
the racial make-up approximately 92 per cent white, seven per cent
black and one per cent of Indian, Hispanic and Asian origins. Its main
cities are Louisville (300,000), Lexington/Fayette (220,000),
Ownsboro (55,000), Covington (50,000) Bowling Green (40,000),
Fort Knox (32,000) and Paducah (30,000). The capital is Frankfort
(population 30,000).

Manufacturing is the state's main industry, with Kentucky renowned
for its coal mining steel, whiskey and tobacco products. Tourism is
another important earner.

My Old Kentucky Home, written by Scots-Irish songwriter Stephen Collins Foster, is the state song for Kentucky.

The entire southern border of Kentucky runs alongside Tennessee; to the east Kentucky faces West Virginia and Virginia; to the west Missouri, and to the north Ohio, Indiana and Illinois.

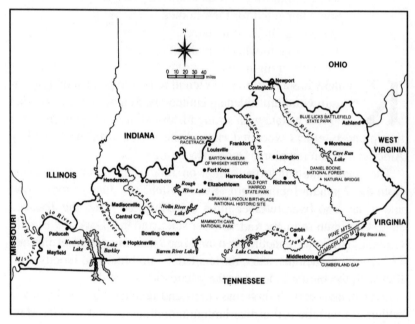

Kentucky

Ode to the Scots-Irish in America

They landed in Pennsylvania
and on to Philadelphia,
Caught the wagon trains
took the Great Wagon Road
and spread out through Virginia
and on to Tennessee,
westward to Missouri on to the Rio Grande.
Some hungered for their homes
like a dog clings to its bones.
They clung to what little that they had
but with strength and strong will
they knew they couldn't stand still
and with all of the dangers they pushed on.

It was 1717
when the first ship set sail,
to take them to a life
in a new world far away.
They were weavers, they were farmers
men of many trades,
they were determined, and hard working, they were brave.
On wooden ships they sailed
many floundered in the gales.
But in their thousands they kept coming
with their Presbyterian faith.
The Ulster-Scots set sail, and
with Bibles in their hands they moved on.

From this Northern Irish race
history would be made,
as they led the battle
for the freedom of the land
When the forces of the Crown
were sent to put them down,
four hundred Virginians turned the force around.

George Washington said,
if defeated everywhere else
I will make my stand for liberty
amongst the Scots-Irish
in my native Virginia.
When the war is over they'll be free.

In the Appalachian mountains
they sat and played their music.
Sang about their journeys
from the old world to the new.
They called them hillbillies
as they played their billy tunes,
built homesteads in the mountains
with the dangers that they knew
They were frontiersmen
who went to defend
Texas at the Alamo
and many died, died there with pride
Davy Crockett's the one you all know.

They gave all they had to America
as they moved to all parts of the land.
In the battles of the Civil War
on both sides they took their stand.
Thirteen U.S. Presidents
came from the Scots-Irish race
The astronaut Edward D. White
was the first American to walk in space.
If they ask you where you came from
walking in the Shenandoah?
Tell them you're Scots-Irish,
you have been here for 250 years or more.

JIM LINDSAY

4

From Ulster *to Pennsylvania and Kentucky*

The Scots-Irish Presbyterian settlers who set up home in American frontier states like Pennsylvania and Kentucky during the 18th century came of families who had moved from lowland Scotland into the Province of Ulster in Ireland in the 17th century plantation.

From 1607, the plantation of Ulster was set in train under the monarchy of James I (or James the Sixth of Scotland) and by 1640 it was estimated that 100,000 Scots and 20,000 English had settled in the Province. The genocide committed against the Protestant population in the 1641 rebellion by the native Irish population stemmed the flow of people from the mainland, but by 1672 the numbers had dramatically increased and the north of Ireland had become a stronghold for the Scottish and English planter stock, with significant English presence in the other parts of the island.

The Presbyterian segment was further augmented by the thousands who fled Scotland during the persecution years under Charles II and James II, both Roman Catholic Stuart monarchs, and by the immigration into Ulster of about 50,000 Scots in the several decades after the triumph by the Protestant King William III at the Battle of the Boyne in 1690.

Down and Antrim - the Ulster regions closest in historical and geographical terms to Scotland - were the most successful counties planted by the Scots, although Tyrone and Donegal were largely given over to Scottish families when the plantation officially began. Armagh and

Fermanagh were prevailingly English settlements, while Londonderry and Cavan showed both influences. Only Monaghan, of the nine Ulster counties, remained truly native Irish, except for one Plantation settlement known as Scotstown. The Plantation lands in Ireland covered territory of 800,000 acres.

The regions of Scotland where most of the new Ulster settlers derived were Galloway, Dunfries, Renfrewshire, Ayrshire, Argyllshire and Lanarkshire in the west and Edinburgh, the Lothians and Berwickshire in the east. A small number came from Aberdeen and Inverness in the north east.

The coast of Ulster and the Scottish shoreline are situated only about 15 miles apart at the nearest points and for centuries since the middle ages the peoples of the two regions have moved regularly across the North Channel for trade and social purposes. In religion, culture, social attitudes and dialect, most people in Ulster and Scotland today share broad common ground.

From the early part of the 17th century, Ulster became a diverse melting pot for peoples from three widely different cultures and backgrounds - the Scottish lowland Presbyterians, the English Anglicans and the native Irish Roman Catholics. Strains were then evident that were to be carried through over almost four centuries to the present day.

Ulster had by the mid-17th century a clear Protestant majority, but this did not necessarily mean that the Presbyterians saw eye to eye with their Anglican neighbours who were members of the Reformed Church of Ireland. There were wide theological differences and cultural and ideological diversities that were difficult to bridge.

With the French Huguenot Protestants, the Ulster Presbyterians were engaged through the 17th century in profitable linen and wool manufacturing industry and in agriculture and, away from the lands, they prospered in the main towns of Belfast, Lisburn, Londonderry, Ballymena and Carrickfergus, assuming top posts of civic and legal responsibility.

However, in 1698 a crisis was precipitated when the English wool merchants persuaded parliament to bar the exportation of Irish products. This came on top of a 1692 edict from Church of England bishops who sat in the Irish parliament which required all office-holders under the Crown to partake of the Lord's Supper three times a year in an Anglican Church.

Severe penalties were imposed on Presbyterian ministers who preached contrary to the guidelines laid down in the Anglican law and prayer books. Defiance of the High Church strictures meant disqualification from their positions as ministers. The non-conformist clergy were unable to sanctify marriage; unable to officiate at the baptism or burial of members of their congregation and prevented from teaching on any aspect of the faith in schools. Presbyterian laymen were unable to hold political office, serve in the military and even bear arms.

Aristocratic landlords also made life very difficult for the peasant farmers by demanding exorbitant rents for the small cottages and holdings dotted around the hillsides of Ulster. Many families turfed out of their homes had no alternative but to up and go to America and the plight of the underclass in the north of Ireland was not helped by the famine of 1740-41 and by the several years of bad harvesting that preceded it.

The dissenting Ulster-Scots Presbyterians were discriminated in their religion, means of employment and social pursuits and this left them deeply resentful and alienated from the political establishment in London, and the aristocratic landlord and church representatives administering the draconian laws in the Province.

Not unexpectedly, the restrictive church laws and practices which were in vogue over several decades well into the 18th century proved the catalyst for the start of the mass movement of the Scots-Irish to the new lands being opened up in the American colonies. From 1717 the exodus from Ulster had begun and for almost the next 100 years an estimated quarter of a million hardy souls were to make the arduous trek across the Atlantic to start a new life in a largely uninhabited wilderness.

Recruiting agents from the North American colonies had been in Ulster from about 1715 strongly advising people that if they emigrated to what was then termed the "New World" they would find lots of free and unclaimed land. The Presbyterian lowlanders who still clung to their Scottish traditions were quick to listen and eagerly the first ships were put into service in 1717.

The first vessel to leave Ulster for America was the Eagle Wing from the little Co. Down port of Groomsport on September 9, 1636.

Some 140 Presbyterians were on board, but, after nearly two months at sea and three-quarters of the way to America, heavy storms forced the severely battered 150-tonne ship to return to Ulster.

Ulster people did make the far Atlantic shores in trickles in the years up to the end of the 17th century, including Co. Donegal pastor the Rev. Francis Makemie, the founding father of the Presbyterian Church in America. But it was not until the spring of 1717 that the first properly organised emigrant passenger ship set sail ... the "Friends Goodwill", embarking from Larne for Boston.

This was to be the signal for the departure of 5,000 immigrants from the Province that year, and, over the next 80 years, they poured out of the ports of Belfast, Larne, Londonderry, Portrush and Newry in simple wooden ships, bound for New York, Philadelphia, New Castle (Delaware), Charleston and Baltimore.

The British authorities placed no obstacles in the way of those Presbyterians keen to move and, initially, most found the Quaker colony of Pennsylvania much more attractive than the strongly Roman Catholic Maryland colony or the Anglican-dominated Virginia. There, the main man to greet them was an urbane Quaker of Ulster birth, James Logan from Lurgan, Co Armagh, who was executive secretary to the colonial chief William Penn.

James Logan initially welcomed the arrival of his fellow-countrymen and women, but he soon tired of their belligerent attitudes and their total disregard for the ground rules of acquiring colonial land, and in 1724 he was referring to them as "these bold and indigent strangers."

Of the first immigrants, some went with valuable possessions and a little cash to lay claim to American land. But many families, from the farm labouring and linen weaving class, had totally impoverished themselves in raising the money for the fare and they were in pretty poor shape, physically and financially, when they reached the other side.

At the time the Pennsylvania Gazette sympathetically explained a main reason for the mass migration from Ulster:

"Poverty, wretchedness, misery and want are becoming almost universal among them; that ... there is not corn enough rais'd for their subsistence one year with another, and at the same time the trade and manufactures of the nation being crampl'd and discourag'd, the labouring people have little to do, and consequently are not able to purchase bread at its present dear rate. That the taxes are nevertheless exceeding heavy, and money very scarce; and add to all this, that their griping, avaricious landlords exercise over them the most merciless racking tyranny and oppression. Hence it is that such swarms of them are driven into America."

There were five great waves of emigration to America from Ulster in the 18th century: 1717-18; 1725-29; 1740-41; 1754-55 and 1771-75, and by the end of the century the Scots-Irish became, next to the English, the most influential of the white population of America. At the time the Scots-Irish segment of the population in the United States was as high as 20 per cent in North Carolina, Kentucky, Tennessee and South Carolina.

Being a people who had been on the move for several centuries, the Scots-Irish Presbyterians felt they had been the victims of discrimination from political, military, economic and religious authority and this developed a siege mentality which they maintained in settling the frontier. Many of those in the first wave of emigration to America had fought for the Williamite cause in the 1688-89 Siege of Derry and in subsequent battles at the Boyne, Aughrim and Enniskillen which confirmed the Protestant succession in Britain.

Loyalty to the family was absolute in the character of the Scots-Irishman and woman and those not of the same breed were looked upon with suspicion and hostility.

Being the first Americans, the Scots-Irish people, unlike the other European ethnic groups of later years, did not have to endure an apprenticeship period when they had to adjust and learn the ways of the indigenous population. When they moved beyond the eastern coastal ports to the Appalachian foothills, they became masters in their homelands and townships and, unchallenged by any other civilised sector, they set the rules and patterns of white society. As the first Americans they were totally assimilated into the fabric of the nation and their principles and virtues are deeply embedded into the constitution of the United States.

The Scots-Irish had to have remarkable natural resources and human capacity to survive the harsh unchartered atmosphere of the American frontier, but it was their tenacity of spirit and solid belief in the rightness of their cause which keep them steadily moving westwards and southwards to new settlements, and fresh challenges.

These people left an indelible mark on the society of eastern and western Pennsylvania, where they were among the earliest of the white settlers after the Quakers.

The Scots-Irish played a highly significant role in the Revolutionary War, prompting one Hessian officer to remark that the American revolution was "nothing more than an Irish-Scotch Rebellion."

A few years after the War, Benjamin Franklin acknowledged that the Ulster immigrants and their children were in possession of the government of Pennsylvania, by "their majority in the Assembly, as well as a great part of the territory."

When they travelled along the Great Wagon Road to the Shenandoah Valley of Virginia and into the Carolinas, Tennessee and Kentucky, the Scots-Irish shaped communities in their likeness and character. And when they reached Oklahoma, Kansas and even California, and went down into Texas via the Rio Grande, the Scots-Irish seal on the lifestyle and psyche of the regions were apparent for all to see.

Not everyone however was complimentary to the Scots-Irish. Federal Congressman and New England traveller of the late 18th century, Uriah Trecy, described them as "the most God-provoking democrats on this side of hell."

Dr. James H. Snowdon, of Pittsburgh, paid this colourful tribute in 1910 to the race of people he was proud to be descended from: "The original Scotch Irishman may be described as a Scotchman who was rubbed through the sieve of Ireland. And therefore he combines in a degree the excellences of both races. He had the Scotch tenacity and obduracy tempered with Irish plasticity, buoyancy and brightness.

" He is a boulder of Scotch granite, overlaid and softened with the green verdure of Ireland. There is a granite in his bones, but his mind is witty and his heart tender. Such is the complex and rich stream of heredity that flowed out of Scotland through Ireland and that still retains strong and fine qualities and courses in its veins."

5

Pillars of society *in Pennsylvania*

Pennsylvania was the favourite American colony for the Scots-Irish immigrants in the first half of the 18th century and their political and social influence in the state was very pronounced over the decades that followed, right into the 20th century.

During the colonial period Lurgan (Co Armagh)-born James Logan, a Quaker, was the leading politician in the province and at various times he held the offices of provincial secretary, commissioner of property, mayor of Philadelphia, acting governor and chief justice.

Pennsylvania was established by English Quakers in 1681 and for a 60-year period the Society of Friends controlled the political and economic life in the state. By 1740, this was no longer the case and due to significant population influx, they were outnumbered by both the Germans and the Scots-Irish. From then until the Revolutionary War period Quaker power in Pennsylvania became increasingly untenable.

During the Revolutionary War period James Smith, George Taylor and Thomas McKean, all men of Ulster stock, were members of the Continental Congress and signatories to the Declaration of Independence in July, 1776, along with Maghera, Co Londonderry-born Charles Thomson, secretary to the Continental Congress and designer of the Great Seal of America.

Joseph Reed and George Bryan served as presidents of Pennsylvania and in the immediate post-Revolutionary War period and William Findley, Robert Whitehall and John Smilie were state representatives.

A survey of politics in Pennsylvania since 1790 confirms that while the Scots-Irish may have been outnumbered in population terms by the English and German settlers, they held a very high share of the important state and civic offices.

James Buchanan, whose family came from Deroran near Omagh in Co Tyrone, was the only Pennsylvanian to move to the White House as President, and he was also a United States senator, Congressman, minister for separate periods to Great Britain and Russia and US Secretary of State. Buchanan was born in Lancaster County, Pennsylvania.

United States cabinet ministers from the Scots-Irish community included William J. Duane, James G. Blaine, John Armstrong, Franklin MacVeagh, Philander C. Knox, Jeremiah S. Black, and Andrew W. Mellon.

Other Scots-Irish national political leaders and statesmen from Pennsylvania were William Maclay, Samuel Maclay, Matthew S. Quay, Robert W. Mackey, A. K. McClure, George Logan, Thomas A. Scott, John W. Morrison, James Rose, Thomas H. Burrows, Daniel Agnew, James Ewing, David Fullerton and Andrew Gregg. The 12 Scots-Irish governors of Pennsylvania were Thomas McKean, William Findley, David R. Porter, William F. Johnston, James Pollock, Andrew G. Gurtin, John W. Geary, John K. Tener, Daniel H. Hastings, Edwin S. Stuart, Robert Pattison and William C. Sproul.

Governor David R. Porter was of a Londonderry family whose father Andrew fought with distinction as a general in the Revolutionary War. General Horace Porter, son of the Governor, was a close aide of General Ulysses Grant on the federal side during the Civil War. With Grant he engaged through the various battles and in the peace treaties that were brokered. In civilian life Horace Porter held considerable business interests, including vice-presidency of the Pullman car company.

It was estimated that by 1790 the Scots-Irish population in Pennsylvania was 80,000, a people who found the region a welcoming haven with liberal institutions, excellent laws, low taxes and a climate, which, although much colder in mid-winter than in Ulster, had the benefit of being much warmer over the rest of the year. The land was extremely fertile and rich limestone soils were to be found to the north and west of Philadelphia.

A great many of the Scots-Irish families moved very quickly on arrival in Pennsylvania in a westerly direction and from the early 1730s they took up residence in the lush Shenandoah Valley of Virginia.

The Scots-Irish were just as prominently involved in the legal and judicial institutions of Pennsylvania. From the revolutionary period to 1900, 25 of the 54 justices of the Supreme Court of Pennsylvania were of this ethnic origin, with a further 16 chief justices in that period.

Across 30 Pennsylvania states, the bench was solidly Scots-Irish, accurately reflecting the penchant among this essentially Presbyterian community for the strict adherence of the law. Philadelphia, the main port, had become the largest town in the American colonies with a population of 23,750 in 1760 which rose to 40,000 by the outbreak of the Revolutionary War in 1776.

Thomas McKean, Pennsylvania Governor in 1799 as a Jeffersonian candidate and a signer of the Declaration of Independence in 1776, was the son of a Londonderry-born immigrant to Pennsylvania whose father had moved to Ulster from Argyllshire during the Scottish Plantation. Thomas studied law in Delaware and he developed a successful practice in Pennsylvania, Delaware and New Jersey. He became deputy attorney general in Pennsylvania; clerk of the assembly and later assembly member. This was to be the stepping stone to Congress, where he served as president.

Increasingly, Thomas McKean became more outspoken against British rule and was one of the more radical members of the Stamp Act Congress in 1765. As justice of the court of common pleas and quarter sessions he ordered the use of unstamped paper, and in 1772 as speaker of the assembly he led the movement for a colonial congress.

McKean was a delegate to the first Continental Congress from Delaware and, while at one stage he was advocating reconciliation with the English colonial rulers, his sympathies became more orientated towards independence. A month after the Declaration of Independence was signed he led a battalion of Philadelphia militia to Perth Amboy to reinforce George Washington's hard-pressed forces.

His commitment to the independent cause was absolute. This proud Ulster-Scot was described as "cold in manner, energetic, independent and vain, yet with ability, candour and honesty."

McKean was hounded by the British so much that he was forced to move his family almost constantly. He served in Congress without pay; his family was kept in hiding; his possessions were eventually taken from him and for a period poverty was his reward.

Matthew Thornton, another of the Declaration of Independence signers, came from Londonderry to Maine with his parents in 1718. He lived at Maine and, after completing medical studies in 1740, started a practice in the Scots-Irish colony of Londonderry in New Hampshire.

It was said that in the several decades leading up to the break with the Crown, Matthew Thornton's career was "a chronicle of revolutionary progress in that part of New England." He joined the Continental Congress in November, 1776 and was belatedly permitted to sign the Declaration.

George Taylor, another Ulsterman who signed the Declaration, was the son of a Presbyterian minister. He settled in Chester county, Pennsylvania in 1736, and prospered as a merchant. His activities on the revolutionary side brought him to prominence in politics and by 1775 he was a militia colonel. He became a delegate to the Continental Congress when it was decided to replace the representative who refused to sign. Taylor signed the document on August 2, 1776.

Edward Rutledge, of Co Tyrone Presbyterian stock, was the governor of South Carolina who played a leading role on drafting the Declaration in 1776. He also engaged as a militia officer during the Revolutionary War.

John Hancock, William Whipple, Robert Paine and Thomas Nelson were other signatories of the Declaration with Scots-Irish links. Hancock, the best known, was the president of Congress and the leading politician of his day in New England. He had family connections to Co. Down. The Nelson home was taken over by the British General Lord Cornwallis as his headquarters, later destroyed by fire and, after years of harassment by Crown forces, Nelson died a bankrupt.

John Dunlap, who moved to work in America from a printing company in the mid-18th century in Strabane, Co Tyrone, had the honour of printing the first copies of the Document. Later in 1784, Dunlap had also the distinction of printing America's first daily newspaper, The Pennsylvania Packet.

Colonel John Nixon was the son of Ulster Presbyterian immigrants and, after inheriting a family shipping business and wharf in

Philadelphia, he became one of the most celebrated personalities of the Revolutionary War period. In 1776, Nixon commanded the defence of Fort Island on the Delaware River and was in a command of the Philadelphia guard. On July 8 in Philadelphia he gave the first public reading of the Declaration of Independence and then headed off for several years of militia duty.

By 1779, Nixon was an auditor of public accounts in Pennsylvania and he helped organise the Bank of Philadelphia, primarily to finance the American army. He personally contributed £5,000 and he was then elevated as a director and president of the Bank of America.

A contemporary of John Nixon in the revolutionary struggle was John McKinly, who moved from the north of Ireland in the mid-18th century to settle in Wilmington, Delaware. McKinly was a doctor who also rose rapidly in civic and militia affairs. He was president and the commander in chief of forces in Delaware. When the British occupied Wilmington in September, 1777, following the Battle of Brandywine, he was taken prisoner and they evacuated him to Philadelphia after the capture of that city.

McKinly was elected to the Continental Congress, but did not serve and after the war he resumed his medical practice in Wilmington.

Of the 56 signatories of the Declaration of Independence on July 4, 1776, 24 were lawyers and jurists, 11 were merchants, nine farmers and the rest large plantation owners, men of means, well-educated. They signed the document knowing well that the penalty would be death if they were captured by the British. Most survived to become leading statesmen and politicians in the new American nation.

News of the signing of the Declaration of Independence was first relayed to the people of Britain by the Belfast News Letter in its edition of August 23-27, 1776. The newspaper had obtained the news exclusively via a communication conveyed on a ship which arrived into the port of Londonderry from America.

Signing of the Declaration of Independence in Philadelphia, July 4, 1776.

6

First settlers *on the Delaware River*

Ulster-Scots were the first white settlers in the Northampton county region of Pennsylvania which lies about 30 miles north of Philadelphia in the vicinity of Allentown. In 1728, John Boyd went with Colonel Thomas Craig, from Philadelphia, to the Forks of the Delaware River alongside New Jersey and put down a stake at the Craig settlement at the springs of Caladaque Creek.

Boyd, who was married to Jane Craig, was followed by fellow countrymen and Presbyterians from the north of Ireland, among them Hugh Wilson and Samuel Brown.

"By 1731, they had accumulated a sufficient community to form a respectable settlement," recalls the Rev John C. Clyde in his "History of the Irish Settlements".

A church was organised there by the Presbytery of Philadelphia, with William and Thomas Craig the congregational leaders.

Hugh Wilson, born in Ireland in 1689, was one of the commissioners appointed to develop the township of Easton. He is claimed by his descendants to have been the son of a Scottish laird and was a man of considerable influence in Northampton county.

A second flank of the Scots-Irish settled was later settled nearby at the mouth of Martin's Creek and at the time German settlers were also moving into the region in large numbers.

In 1752 when Northampton county was organised, there were nearly 6,000 white inhabitants: about 4,000 Germans, 800 Scots-Irish, 300 Dutch and several hundred French Huguenots. The Germans had gradually supplanted the Scots-Irish through the entire valley of Kittatinny, from Easton to Maryland, as the increasingly restless Ulster folk set their sights on other territories, notably the Shenandoah Valley of Virginia and the Carolinas.

Northampton county is said to be unsurpassed by any other region in Eastern Pennsylvania in fertility of soil and climate. But, tragically, the county was a theatre of battle during the French/Indian wars of 1754-63 and the white settlers bore the brunt of frequent attacks by native American tribesmen on their stockades.

Interestingly, in Northampton county today there is a Belfast township, and a Bangor, as in Northern Ireland.

Robert Parke, a Pennsylvanian Quaker, in a letter to his sister in Ireland in 1725, wrote that land in the region is of all prices. "Even from ten pounds to one hundred pounds a hundred, according to the goodness or else of the situation thereof, and grows dearer every year by reason of vast quantities of people that come here yearly from several parts of the world; therefore thee and thy family or any that I wish well would desire to make what speed you can to come here the sooner the better.

"This country yields extraordinary increase of all sorts of grain likewise . . . so that it as plentiful a country as any can be if people will be industrious . . . all sorts of provisions are extraordinary plenty in Philadelphia market where county people bring in their commodities.

"This country abounds in fruit, scarce an house but has an apple, peach and cherry orchard, as for chestnuts, walnuts and hazelnuts, strawberries, billberrys and mullberrys they grow wild in the woods and fields in vast quantities."

Incredibly, considering the distance and the turbulent waters of the Atlantic Ocean, very few emigrant ships from Ulster were lost at sea during the 18th century. According to Illustrated London News only three are recorded lost.

Many emigrants experienced the terror of violent storms with some lost overboard and others dying from disease, picked up in the crowded holds and cabins of the wooden vessels. The journey from Ulster to America lasted from six to 10 weeks.

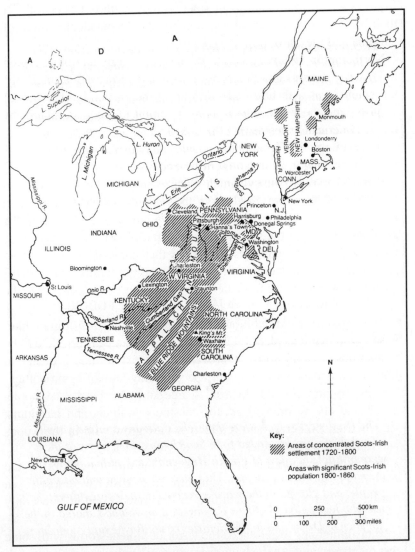

Settlement and Migration of Scots-Irish in North America

"

Twenty thousand Protestants left Ulster on the destruction of the woollen trade. Many more were driven away by the first passage of the Test Act. The stream had slackened, in the hope that the law would be altered. When the prospect was finally closed, men of spirit and energy refused to remain; . . . and thence forward, until . . . 1782, annual shiploads poured themselves out of Belfast and Londonderry. The resentment which they carried with them continued to burn in their new homes; and in the War of Independence, England had no fiercer enemies than the grandsons and great-grandsons of the Presbyterians who had held Ulster against Tyrconnell.

"

19th century historian JAMES ANTHONY ROUDE
(The English in Ireland, 1872)

"

The Presbyterian Irish were themselves already a mixed people. Though mainly descended from Scotch ancestors, many of them were of English, a few of French Huguenot, and quite a number of them old Milesian extraction. They were a truculent and obstinate people, and gloried in the warlike renown of their forefathers, the men who had followed Oliver Cromwell, and who had shared in the defence of Derry and in the victories of the Boyne and Aughrim.

"

PRESIDENT THEODORE ROOSEVELT

7

President with *integrity and zeal*

James Buchanan, the only United States President born in Pennsylvania, was the son of an Ulster Presbyterian merchant whose family lived in Deroran near Omagh in Co Tyrone and who emigrated from Co Londonderry to America in 1783. Born into a family of 11, Buchanan had Ulster-Scots links on both sides of the family — his mother was Elizabeth Speer, a well-read and highly intelligent daughter of an immigrant farmer.

James Buchanan Sen. exerted a strong influence over his statesman-to-be son and in later years the President wrote: "My father was a man of practical judgment, and of great industry and perseverance. He was a kind father, a sincere friend, and an honest and religious man."

Buchanan's mother was also a devout Christian, one whose competitive arguments with her son provided the edge which allowed him to successfully develop legal and political careers. Of his mother he wrote: "I attribute my little distinction which I may have acquired in the world to the blessing which He conferred upon me in granting me such a mother."

James Buchanan was born in a log cabin at Stony Batter in Cove Gap, Franklin county, Pennsylvania in 1791 and, when the family moved to Mercersburg, he studied Greek and Latin at the Old Stone Academy in between working in his father's trading store. After graduation, he studied law in Lancaster, then the Pennsylvanian state capital, and was admitted to the Bar in 1812.

Like his father, James Buchanan was a federalist and he was nominated for the state assembly on August 4, 1814, the same day the British were burning the White House during their occupation of Washington. This resulted in a brief military involvement, but Buchanan's career edged towards politics and his 1857-61 term as President came at one of the most critical times in American history.

Before reaching the White House he had spent 42 years in public life as a Democratic state assemblyman, US representative, minister to Russia, secretary of state and minister to Britain. But as the 15th President he was confronted with the national dilemma of the 1850s slavery wrangle, and he also had to contend with urban expansion across the states, a dramatic increase in immigration, economic problems and competition from the developing Republican Party.

Buchanan, an imposing six-foot figure, was the only bachelor to reach the Presidency, although he was engaged to Ann Coleman, the daughter of a wealthy Pennsylvanian ironmaster.

Ann died suddenly after terminating the engagement and the tragedy deeply affected Buchanan, then a Pennsylvanian state assemblyman. He became a close associate of President Andrew Jackson, who appointed him as minister to Russia in 1832.

Later, in 1844, Buchanan was appointed by President James Knox Polk as his secretary of state and, at a time of great territorial expansion, he was instrumental in settling the Oregon territory and acquiring southwestern lands from Mexico.

Under President Franklin Pierce in 1852, he became minister to Britain and, when he returned home four years later, his turn had come for the Presidency. He was elected with 45 per cent of the popular vote and 59 per cent support from the electoral college.

America had become embroiled in the great slavery debate, triggered by the Kansas-Nebraska Act which pushed the black slaves into the new territories. Buchanan, although opposed personally to slavery, supported the unpopular legislation through Congress and it made him many enemies.

A successful foreign policy, aimed at advancing American influence in Central and South America and China and Japan, failed to push the slavery issue off centre stage and his Presidential term ended on a low note for the 70-year-old veteran who became depressed by the nation's slide into civil war. His Republican successor was Abraham Lincoln, a man of destiny whose life was taken near the end of a long and bitter struggle.

Buchanan returned to his beloved Wheatland estate in Lancaster, Pennsylvania, worn-out by the rigours of high office. However, he continued as a member of the House of Representatives until he was 77, having served on that body for 47 years. He died on June 1, 1868 and his funeral attracted 20,000 people.

James Buchanan, whose orphaned niece Harriet Lane served as official White House hostess during the Presidency, was an active Presbyterian and a strict Sabbatarian. He recited daily prayers and was thoroughly familiar with the Bible. However, he did not formally belong to a church until he retired from the Presidency - joining the Presbyterian congregation at Lancaster.

His youngest brother the Rev Edward Young Buchanan was rector of Trinity Episcopal Church in Philadelphia and married Ann Eliza Foster, sister of the renowned composer Stephen Collins Foster, whose family had also emigrated from Ulster.

Republican President Ulysses S. Grant said of James Buchanan in 1885: "In 1856 I preferred the success of a Presidential candidate whose election would prevent or postpone secession of the states, to seeing the country plunged into a war the end of which no man could foretell. With a Democrat elected by the unanimous vote of the slave states there could be no pretext for secession for four years. I therefore voted for James Buchanan as President."

Buchanan said as early as 1826: "I believe slavery to be a great political and a great moral evil. I thank God my lot has been cast in a state where it does not exist."

And to his successor Abraham Lincoln, he said: "My dear Sir, if you are as happy on entering the White House as I am on leaving, you are a happy man indeed."

Fateful words indeed, as events were to unfold over four years of turmoil in the Civil War during which President Lincoln was tragically to pay for his involvement in the running of the nation's affairs with his life.

★★★

THE THIRTEEN SCOTS-IRISH PRESIDENTS:

About one-third of the 41 United States Presidents are of Scots-Irish Presbyterian ancestry and their achievements in this highest office are testimony of a people who have contributed much to the American nation from its very inception.

- **ANDREW JACKSON:** (Democrat - 7th President 1829-37). Born on March 15, 1767 in the Waxhaw region of North Carolina, his family left Ulster in 1765, having lived in the village of Boneybefore near Carrickfergus in Co Antrim. Andrew distinguished himself as a lawyer, soldier, politician and statesman.

- **JAMES KNOX POLK:** (Democrat - 11th President 1845-49). Born on November 2, 1797 near Charlotte in North Carolina, he is descended from a Robert Polk (Pollok) of Londonderry, who arrived in the American colonies in 1680. James Knox Polk was a Governor of Tennessee before making it to the White House.

- **JAMES BUCHANAN:** (Democrat - 15th President 1857-61). Born on April 23, 1791 in Mercersburg, Pennsylvania, he was brought up in a Presbyterian home like his two predecessors Jackson and Polk. The family came originally from Deroran near Omagh, Co Tyrone and they left Londonderry for America in 1783.

- **ANDREW JOHNSON:** (Democrat - 17th President 1865-69). Born on December 28, 1808 in Raleigh, North Carolina, his name-sake and grandfather from Mounthill outside Larne in Co Antrim came to America about 1750. Andrew rose to the Presidency from humble log cabin roots and he worked as a tailor for many years in Greeneville, Tennessee before he made it as mayor of the town and as a national politician and a statesman.

- **ULYSSES SIMPSON GRANT:** (Republican -18th President 1869-77). Born April 27, 1822, Ulysses Grant was the man who commanded the Union Army in the American Civil War. His mother Hannah Simpson was descended from the Simpson family of

Dergenagh near Dungannon, Co Tyrone. His great-grandfather John Simpson left Ulster for America in 1760. Ulysses was a Methodist.

- **CHESTER ALAN ARTHUR:** (Republican - 21st President 1881-85). Born on October 5, 1830 in Fairfield, Vermont, his grandfather and father, Baptist pastor William Arthur, emigrated to the United States from Dreen near Cullybackey in Co Antrim in 1801. President Arthur was an Episcopalian.

- **GROVER CLEVELAND:** (Democrat - 22 and 24th President 1885-89 and 1893-97). Born on March 8, 1837 in Caldwell, New Jersey, his maternal grandfather Abner Neal left Co Antrim in the late 18th century. Grover was the son of a Presbyterian minister and he belonged that denomination.

- **BENJAMIN HARRISON:** (Republican - 23rd President 1889-93). Born on August 20, 1833 at North Bend, Ohio. Two of his great grandfathers James Irwin and William McDowell were Ulster immigrants. Benjamin was a Presbyterian.

- **WILLIAM McKINLEY** (Republican 25th President - 1897-1901). Born on January 29, 1843 in Niles, Ohio, he was the great-grandson of James McKinley, who emigrated to America from Conagher, near Ballymoney in Co Antrim about 1743. William McKinley, a Methodist, was assassinated at Buffalo, New York on September 6, 1901.

- **WOODROW WILSON:** (Democrat - 28th President 1913-21). Born on December 28, 2856 in Staunton, Virginia, Woodrow was the grandson of James Wilson, who emigrated to North Carolina from Dergalt, Co Tyrone about 1807. Woodrow's father, Dr Joseph Ruggles Wilson, was a Presbyterian minister and he belonged to that denomination.

- **RICHARD MILLHOUSE NIXON:** (Republican - 37th President 1969-74). Born on January 13, 1913 in Yorba Linda, California, Richard Nixon had Ulster connections on two sides of his family.

His Nixon ancestors left Co Antrim for America around 1753, while the Millhouses came from Carrickfergus and Ballymoney, also in Co Antrim. He died in 1994. President Nixon was a Quaker.

- **JAMES EARL CARTER:** (Democrat - 39th President 1976-81). Born on October 1, 1924 in Plains, Georgia. Scots-Irish settler Andrew Cowan, the great grandfather of President Jimmy Carter's great grandmother of his father's side, was one of the first residents of Boonesborough in South Carolina in 1772. Andrew Cowan was a Presbyterian, Jimmy Carter is a Baptist.

- **WILLIAM JEFFERSON CLINTON:** (Democrat - 41st President 1993-). Born on August 19, 1946 in Hope, Hempstead County, Arkansas. Bill Clinton claims to be five times removed from Lucas Cassidy who left Co Fermanagh for America around 1750. Lucas Cassidy was of Presbyterian stock, President Clinton is a Baptist. He is the only serving US President to have visited Northern Ireland.

★★★

- **JOHN C. CALHOUN,** the son of Co. Donegal-born Presbyterian Patrick Calhoun, was Vice-President to John Quincy Adams (1825-29) and Andrew Jackson (1829-32). Calhoun was born into a log cabin settlement in the South Carolina Piedmont area and he rose to become one of the most influential statesmen and politicians in the American South in the first half of the 19th century. Calhoun served in the South Carolina state legislature and the US Congress and Senate over a period of more than 40 years. He wrote two books "Disquisition of Government" and "A Discourse on the Constitution and Government of the United States." These set out a conservative political philosophy that was a marker for very many Americans then and since.

8

Presbyterian witness *at Donegal Springs*

Donegal Presbyterian Church near Lancaster in eastern Pennsylvania was the focal point for one of the earliest Scots-Irish settlements on American soil, the congregation being established as early as 1721. Co Donegal in north west Ireland was the homeland of the first families who moved inland from Philadelphia to set up homes on the Indian-titled territory of Chiquesalunga, fertile but largely wilderness lands hitherto only inhabited by the native American tribes.

Presbyterianism was taken to America by Donegal pastor the Rev Francis Makemie in 1683 and in 1706 he founded the Philadelphia Presbytery, the first independent church body of any kind in the 'New World' colonies. By 1717, there were 13 organised Presbyterian churches in the region and, although many Glasgow and Edinburgh-educated clerics arrived from Ulster and Scotland on the immigrant ships, they could not meet the growing demands of new congregations that were sprouting up as the frontier was pushed westwards.

The earliest documented evidence of a Presbyterian congregation at Donegal Springs was contained in a letter dated August 1, 1721, dispatched by Andrew Galbraith to the Presbytery of New Castle in Delaware. In the letter, Galbraith asked that a minister be sent to supply the people at "Chickens Longus" (his spelling version of the word Chiquesalunga). Supply ministers were sent, but without adequate guides in the rugged frontier terrain they lost their way and never appeared.

The first full-time pastor appointed was Scottish-born the Rev James Anderson, who had worked in America since 1709 and supplied a New York city pulpit before the call in August, 1727 to the log cabin meeting house at Donegal Springs, alongside the Susquehanna River and bountiful Springs.

A stone church was erected in 1730 to replace the log cabin, the stone gathered by the men and women of the congregation from the quarries and fields nearby. Tradition in the area relates that the women drove the wagon which carried the stones to the site of the building, and that the old horse which pulled the wagon died just as the last stone was placed at the peak of the hip-roofed structure. As a gesture of gratitude for faithful service, the horse's head was buried under the pulpit.

The first Donegal stone church was erected similar to the church at Rathneedy near Donegal town in Ireland, the first Presbyterian meeting house built for and by the people of that county in 1674. A cemetery was started soon after the Donegal Springs church became established, and a school was up and running within a short period.

The first gravestone in the cemetery belongs to Thomas Jamison, who died in 1732. The Rev Colin McFarquhar, church minister during the Revolutionary War, is buried there beside his wife Elizabeth, as is Colonel Alexander Lowrey, who led a battalion of militia from the church to the Brandywine in 1777.

Colonel Lowrey was one of the first in the region to advocate independence. He was a delegate to Carpenter's Hall in Philadelphia, where the resolution in favour of independence was passed on June 16. 1776. A contemporary, Colonel Bertram Galbraith, raised a battalion in 1775 composed entirely of Donegalians and a number were killed or taken prisoner at the battle of Long Island.

Other members of Donegal Presbyterian Church who distinguished themselves in battle during the Revolutionary War were Lieutenant Colonel William Clark, Captain Hugh Pedan, Captain Alexander Boggs, Quartermaster Sergeant David Jamison and his brother John, Captain Zachariah Moore, Captain James Anderson, Captain Joseph Work, Captain Nathaniel Lyttle, Captain Joseph Lyttle, Captain Alexander Scott and Captain Robert C. Craig.

It was Lurgan-born James Logan, the agent for Governor William Penn in Pennsylvania, who reserved all of Donegal township for the

Scots-Irish. The township was later divided into Rapho, Mount Joy, East and West Donegal, and Convoy townships, all named after locations in Co Donegal back in Ireland. It included what are now the boroughs of Elizabethtown, Marietta and Mount Joy.

James Logan, who counted "considerable numbers of good sober people" among the heavy Ulster migration, allowed very few land grants in any place after 1720, largely as a result of the disarray after the death of William Penn in 1718. An exception was made in the case of the Scots-Irish people who he said, "If kindly used, will, I believe, be orderly as they have hitherto been, and easily dealt with; they will also, I expect be a leading example to others."

The grants were confirmed for the settlement at Donegal.

Samuel Evans in his history of Lancaster County (1883) refers to Donegal as "one of the most remarkable Scotch-Irish settlements in America", while Wayland Dunaway in 'The Scotch-Irish of Colonial Pennsylvania' states that "Donegal was a major nursery of Scotch-Irish Presbyterianism." The Encyclopedia of the Presbyterian Church of America (1884) says of Donegal Church: "Of several Scotch-Irish settlements in America, the one in Donegal township, Lancaster County, Pennsylvania was the most notable. It became the nursery of Presbyterianism in middle, western and southwestern Pennsylvania, and of Virginia and North Carolina."

Members of the congregation of Donegal Presbyterian Church in 1722 from the records of the Presbytery of New Castle, Delaware were: Richard, James and John Allison; William Braines; Thomas and John Black; James Brownie; William and Robert Bohannon; Patrick Campbell; James Cunningham; Jonas Davenport; James, John and Andrew Galbraith; George Gray; Thomas Gale; John Gardner; Samuel Fulton; James, Albert and John Henricks; Henry Henrickson; Gordon Howard; Alexander Hutchinson; John C. and Michael Ker; James Kile; Robert, William and George Mitchell; Robert, William and George Middleton; John McDaniel; Column MacHenry; Robert Monday; John Miller; Samuel and James Smith; James Patterson (the Indian trader); George Stewart; John Sterer; Robert and Thomas Wilkins; Joseph Work; William Walker and Michael Wood.

Samuel Fulton was a typical Ulster pioneer settler at Donegal township, taking up residence on 309 acres of land at old Peter's Road, about a mile from the Donegal meeting house. He married Elizabeth

Stewart, daughter of George and Jean Stewart, who also belonged to the Church, and they had three sons and a daughter.

The humble Fulton stone cabin, probably built around 1724, was still standing in 1997, and, after it was purchased by the trustees of the Ulster-American Folk Park at Omagh in Co Tyrone, the building was dismantled stone by stone and transported across the Atlantic for re-siting at the Omagh theme park.

In 1724, Samuel Fulton's name appeared for the first time on a Donegal township tax assessment and in 1737 he filed a survey with the Pennsylvania land office for a tract of 309 acres. He continued to hold this land until his death in 1760.

The normal procedure for acquiring land in Pennsylvania at that time began with a warrant issued by the land officer and, after a survey, a patent or title deed was issued in the name of the colony proprietor William Penn or his heirs. The patent obliged the new owner to pay the Penn family one shilling sterling for every 100 acres each year, but in almost every respect the settler was a freeholder.

Many settlers allowed 30 years or more to elapse between their first and last step in the process of taking title to their land so as to avoid paying the full purchase price and other costs involved. Since land held by warrant could be purchased and sold as readily as patented lands, they were under no pressure to move.

Donegal township settlers had added reasons to delay. Most of them settled there during the years after William Penn's death in 1718 when the land office was closed and regular procedures were put in abeyance. A few took up lands on the authority of a warrant, but most had no legal rights to settle on Penn lands.

A protracted dispute between the settlers and James Logan, the Penn family's agent, over terms he had promised them for purchasing land led to a block on any surveys being carried out until a settlement was reached. Logan wrote to the Penns in 1727, pointing out that the Germans and the Scots-Irish "frequently sit down on any spot of vacant land they can find, without asking questions." He added: "Both groups pretend that they will pay, but not one in twenty has anything to pay with."

It was a frustrated Thomas Penn who noted in 1734 that the Donegal settlers had been living on his land for "12 or 15 years" and had "paid no consideration for that favour" or made any effort to regularise their tenure. Very definitely a case of squatting on land that did not belong to them, but the Scots-Irish were undeterred!

Many had crossed the Atlantic with little or no money and most lacked the finance to pay even the small amounts demanded by the Penns. The earliest advertisements offered lots of five thousand acres at a purchase price of only £100, with a quit-rent of one shilling for each 100 acres. Even at these prices the land was beyond the means of a good number of the immigrants who had left the north of Ireland to escape poverty.

Samuel Fulton, in his will in 1760, left 170 acres and "the house I dwell in" to his son James. He bequeathed the remaining 139 acres to his son Samuel. James was to bear half the cost of building "a square log house 28 feet by 20 and a storey and a half with a stone chimney", presumably for Samuel's use. The third son John was given a house and four acres of cleared land, two acres from each brother, but only for a year.

Within a year Samuel Fulton Jun. had passed the 139 acres to his brother James and, by 1767, the land was mortgaged to another Donegal family.

James Fulton, of Donegal township, kept a store which sold a variety of goods such as rum, molasses, sugar, rice, wine and cloth. He had a wagon and a team of horses to transport the merchandise and barrels of liquor to the various townships on the eastern Pennsylvanian frontier. A kinsman of the same name was a prosperous general merchant in Philadelphia, representing a company in the north of Ireland, which comprised of Ephraim Campbell, of Londonderry, and his own brother John Fulton, of Ramelton in Co Donegal.

They imported linens and general merchandise and exported flaxseed, staves and flour. James Fulton, of Philadelphia, also invested in iron manufacturing and his company owned ships which carried emigrants from Londonderry to Philadelphia in the 1760s, among them many servants and redemptioners.

The Fultons of Donegal, both James and John, worked closely in business with the Fultons of Philadelphia, and likewise with the Fultons back in the hills and homelands of Londonderry and Donegal. They became one of the most prosperous family names in Pennsylvania, like many of their kinsmen who made the American frontier lands their home.

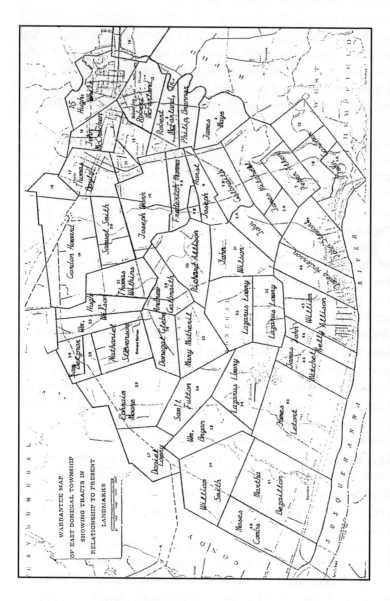

Warrantee Map of East Donegal Township showing tracts in relationship to present landmarks

9

Migration for *reasons of poverty*

D uring the 30 years up to 1750 as many as 12,000 Ulster immigrants arrived in Pennsylvania every year from their homeland, making the colony a stronghold for Scots-Irish settlements and the Presbyterian Church.

In November, 1729, Franklin's Gazette in America summarised the reasons for the migration:

"The English papers have of late been frequent in their accounts of the unhappy circumstances of the common people of Ireland; that poverty, wretchedness , misery and want are become almost universal among them; that there is not corn enough raised for their subsistence one year with another; and, at the same time the trade and manufactures of the nation being cramp'd and discourag'd, the labouring people have little to do, and consequently are not able to purchase bread at its present dear rate: that the taxes are nevertheless exceeding heavy, and money very scarce; and add to all this, that their griping avaricious landlords exercise over them the most merciless racking tyranny and oppression. Hence it is that such swarms of them are driven over into America."

In September, 1736, 1,000 Scots-Irish families sailed from Belfast to Pennsylvania because of their failure to renew land leases on satisfactory terms. These families settled in the eastern and middle counties of Pennsylvania, bringing with them a hatred of the kind of government and high church oppression they faced back in their homeland and a desire to achieve their independence in the new lands on the American frontier.

In 1784, the Scots-Irish percentage of the population in the West Branch Valley of Pennsylvania, known as the Fair Play territory, was 48.75, compared with 20 per cent English, 15 per cent German, 6.25 Scottish, 5 per cent Irish, 2.5 per cent Welsh and 2.5 per cent French Huguenot. The Scots-Irish families in West Branch Valley had moved from Chester, Cumberland, Dauphin and Lancaster counties in the east of the state.

Land problems in both availability and cost caused many Scots-Irish families to migrate southwards to Virginia and South and North Carolina from about 1730 onwards. At the beginning of the 18th century, the price of land in Pennsylvania was £2 per hundred acres. By 1713 it had risen to £10 and in 1732 to £15.

The average farm for a family was about 50 acres, costing in 1732 the then princely sum of seven pounds, ten shillings. But in North Carolina property was on offer at a rate of five shillings per hundred acres and many Pennsylvania families did not require much persuasion to head down the Great Wagon Road to the new lands.

The migrant drift of the Scots-Irish in Pennsylvania to the south and west caused the state's Provincial Council in 1755 to ask: "Was it ever known that any people came from Virginia to purchase here on account of the superior goodness or convenience of our land? On the contrary, have not many thousands of families gone from hence thither? Have not thousands left us to settle in Carolina?

"Has not the exorbitant price at which the proprietors held their lands, and their neglect of Indian purchasing in order to keep up that price, driven these people from us? But they are gone, and gone forever, and numbers are going after them."

10

Revengeful acts *on the Pennsylvanian frontier*

The Derry and Londonderry townships in eastern Pennsylvania were established in the mid-1720s by settlers who moved from the north west part of Ulster. The territory, which lies in the general vicinity of present-day Lancaster and Elizabethtown and about 15 miles from Harrisburg, was good fertile land for the early settler and within a few years of the first emigrant arrivals it became very densely populated.

Derry Presbyterian Church in Dauphin County was established about 1725 by the Scots-Irish settlers and the log-cabin meeting house was a familiar landmark on the line of the Lebanon Valley. The church was founded by the Rev Robert Evans, a frontier missionary, and the first regular minister was the Rev William Bertram.

Two other neighbouring Presbyterian churches - Paxtang (Paxton) and Hanover - were early Scots-Irish domains, with kinsman the Rev John Elder holding the pastorate at Paxtang for 50 years from 1838 at an annual salary of sixty pounds. From 1742 he also held the pastorate at Derry Church and was described as a most efficient shepherd of his extensive charges.

During the French and Indian wars of 1754-63 the region sustained some bloody Indian attacks and the Rev John Elder and his colleagues had to have rifles always at the ready as they preached.

On one occasion in 1756, the Paxtang meeting house was surrounded during a service, but historical accounts say the Indians retreated after their spies had counted the rifles in the hands of the worshippers.

Later in the same year the Indians arrived with the purpose of attacking the worshippers in church, but they arrived on Monday instead of Sunday when the services were normally held. They hung about for several days, before leaving with several prisoners and a number of killings committed.

However, all the murderous atrocities committed were not on the one side and in the winter of 1763-64 there was the notorious "Paxton Boys" affair, when a group of Scots-Irish settlers took the law into their own hands with bloody revengeful killings of Indian tribesmen at Lancaster and Conestoga, the region which gave its Indian name to the traditional frontier covered wagon.

About 50 of the Scots-Irish community at Paxtang, led by a Matthew Smith, carried out the two bloody forays in December, 1763, striking first at the Indian settlement of Conestoga and killing six of the tribe. Later, they killed 14 survivors of the first raid, breaking into Lancaster jail and putting to death Indian men, women and children.

The Paxton killings caused much revulsion among the Quaker civic leaders in Pennsylvania, with the Presbyterian pastor John Elder and his people seriously indicted over the affair. With the wholehearted approval of the Pennsylvania assembly, Governor John Penn placed a substantial reward on the Paxton leaders' heads and called for their capture and removal to Philadelphia for trial.

Many of the Scots-Irish settlers, however, were in no mood to be rebuked or threatened with the law over the killings. They argued that their frontier settlements had been left largely unprotected by their political masters among the pacifist Quaker fraternity in Philadelphia. They perceived that the government was supporting the Indians with funds that could have used by the white settlers for adequate frontier defence.

Quakers from their earliest arrival in America set out to deal with the native Indian tribes as friends and equals. All land on which settlement was likely to occur was purchased from the tribes in negotiations, for a fair price.

The Quaker government in Philadelphia did not feel the need to build forts, establish militia or train scouts and Indian fighters. Their religious convictions and moral conscience demanded that they co-exist peacefully with the native inhabitants. German settlers in Pennsylvania were also inclined, like the English Quakers, to retire rather than fight the Indians. Not so the Scots-Irish!

The Scots-Irish Presbyterians were certainly not as benevolent to the Indian tribes from they first arrived on American soil and, as they pushed the frontier westwards over the next 150 years, the conflict led to much bloodshed on both sides. The possession and dispossession of land was the kernel of the problem.

This uncompromising standpoint was reflected in the defiant mood of the disaffected backwoodsmen from Paxtang and Matthew Smith and a James Gibson led them on a march on Philadelphia to present their grievances before the Quaker-dominated legislature. Before reaching Philadelphia, they were intercepted by four assemblymen led by Benjamin Franklin, who promised immediate government relief if the marchers returned home.

Smith and Gibson outlined the frontier grievances at length, with the chief complaint concerning inequality of Scots-Irish backcountry representation in the Philadelphia assembly.

John Penn was still anxious to proceed with lawful proceedings against those responsible for the Conestoga and Lancaster murders, but the settlers claimed it was improper to "deprive British subjects of their known privileges" if the trials were to take place outside the counties of residence of the defendants.

The Paxton vigilantes blamed the Quakers for the bloody state of the frontier, asserting they were left entirely to themselves to counter hostile attacks from Indian tribes. The issues of properly administering justice to those guilty of the killings and, paradoxically, the defence of the white settlements were not effectively dealt with in the assembly deliberations which followed.

As a result, Governor Penn found it politically expedient to ignore the assembly demands for the immediate prosecution of the Paxton Boys and no one was ever charged for the killings.

A series of anonymous pamphlets were published at the time which acted as an apology for the actions of the Paxton Boys. One headlined: "The conduct of the Paxton-men, impartially represented; the distresses of the frontiers, and the complaints and sufferings of the people fully stated."

The Paxton Boys, led by Matthew Smith and James Gibson, remained unrepentant over the Indian killings. They saw the native American tribes as a threat to their very existence on the frontier lands and, with no proper defences on offer from the government, they felt perfectly justified in taking the law into their own hands.

This was a view generally shared by the Scots-Irish frontiersmen and women of the day; the justice of an eye for an eye during a violent period in America history when Indian life obviously counted for much less than the rights of the white settler.

Political realignments emerged over the next few years between eastern proprietary interests in the Philadelphia assembly and the Scots-Irish Presbyterians and this alliance continued to challenge the Quaker domination of the Pennsylvania assembly for the remainder of the colonial period. Some of the Paxton Boys became closely involved in Pennsylvania politics, joining other immigrant groups in a major land controversy between Connecticut and Pennsylvania, known as the Wyoming Valley dispute.

A decade later when the Revolutionary War started, the men of Paxton, it was said, went into the conflict seeking independence "with heart and soul", and at Boston, Quebec and Yorktown they "fought, bled and died for liberty." And one hundred years later in the American Civil War, their descendants fought with valour on both sides of the divide.

Quaker influence in American society virtually disappeared after the Revolutionary War. The Quakers, as pacifists, refused to take up arms when the War began in 1776, just as they had early refused to engage in the earlier conflict with the Indians, and many of their leaders were held in custody in Virginia by the American patriots.

The Scots-Irish Presbyterians from Pennsylvania through to the Shenandoah Valley, who were aggressively in the vanguard of the struggle for independence, were particularly hostile to those who had once been their landlords and political masters.

Pacifism was not a virtue expounded by the Scots-Irish and, while other religious sects like the Mennonites, Amishmen and Sabbatarians were also against bearing arms in battle, it was the Quakers who faced most vitriol from those committed to ending British rule in America.

The Quakers had been in America since 1681 when William Penn founded the colony in Pennsylvania on lands given to his family by King Charles 11, and the level of patronage and power they exercised for a period of almost 100 years from a Philadelphia base was disproportionate to their numbers. The new predicament they faced was quite an agonising ordeal and even with the British there was a lack of understanding and sympathy for them in their plight.

When the War ended and following George Washington's inauguration as President of the United States, the Quakers of Pennsylvania, New Jersey, Maryland and Virginia sent him an address of welcome from their 1789 yearly convocation.

They pointed out: "We can take no part in warlike measures on any occasions or under any power, but we are bound in conscience to lead quiet and peaceable lives, in Godliness and honesty among men. We are a people whose principles and conduct have been misrepresented and traduced, but we assure you of our loyalty to the new nation."

George Washington replied: "Your principles and conduct are well known to me and it is doing the people called Quakers no more than justice to say that, except their declining to share with others in the burdens of common defence, there is no demonination among us, who are more exemplary and useful citizens.

"I assure you very especially that in my opinion the conscientious scruples of all men should be treated with great delicacy and tenderness; and it is my wish and desire that the laws may always be as extensively accommodated by them, as a due regard to the protection and essential interest of the nation may justify and permit."

Washington's pledge was upheld; the Quakers were molested no more and they were allowed to retreat to the peace of their own communities as rightful citizens of the new American nation. Today, the Quaker community in the United States is very small, concentrated mainly in a few eastern seaboard regions.

George Washington's *First Cabinet*

George Washington's first Cabinet in the initial U.S. Government of 1789 contained four members. Two of them were Scots, Andrew Hamilton of New York, and John Blair of Virginia, and one Ulster-Scot, Henry Knox of Massachussetts.

Among the first Governors for the new State Government set up by the 13 colonies, nine (two-thirds) were of either Scottish or Ulster-Scots origin: George Clinton (New York), Thomas McKean (Pennsylvania), William Livingston (New Jersey), Patrick Henry (Virginia), John MacKinley (Delaware), Richard Caswell (North Carolina), John Rutledge (South Carolina), Archibald Bulloch (Georgia) and Jonathan Trumbull (Connecticut).

Unsympathetic *to Protestantism*

Reports regularly published in the Belfast News Letter demonstrate how closely the ideal of American liberty was linked to the Calvinist Reformed faith. The edition of January 20-24, 1775   contains the text of an appeal to the people of Massachusetts Bay signed by John Hancock and approved by the Continental Congress. It said: "The general tenor of our intelligence from Great Britain, with the frequent reinforcements of the army and navy at Boston, excites the strongest jealousy that the system of colony administration so unfriendly to the Protestant religion, and destructive of American liberty, is still to be pursued, and attempted with force to be carried into execution."

11

Ulster influences *at First Pittsburgh*

The spiritual witness at First Pittsburgh Presbyterian Church in Pennsylvania has been in vogue for 225 years largely due to the firm declaration for the faith by its Ulster-born founders, ministers and subsequent congregations comprised largely of people of the same ethnic origin.

First Pittsburgh Church was established as a congregation under the authority of the Donegal Presbytery in Pennsylvania in April, 1773 with two New England ministers the Rev David McClure and the Rev Levi Frisbie tasked with the initial pastorate. Both had ridden 700 miles on horseback to assume their new charge, which also included a mission to the Indian tribes on the Muskingum River in Ohio.

Church influences in Pittsburgh began in 1761 when the location was known as Fort Pitt. Quaker merchant James Kenny set up a church school in an area that was constantly besieged by hostile Indian tribes and, for a time, Londonderry-born army chaplain Charles Beatty was a popular preacher to the settlers. With another Ulsterman of Huguenot stock as his associate, the Rev George Duffield, the Beatty Presbyterian mission was instrumental in the calls for a permanent church at this far-flung frontier outpost.

Beatty left the north of Ireland in 1729 as a 14-year-old boy with his widowed mother and he earned a living as peddler, tramping from log cabin to log cabin with his wares on his back. It was through the influence of Scots-Irish preacher the Rev William Tennent that he turned to religion and after his ordination as a Presbyterian minister he enlisted as a British army chaplain during their successful assault on Fort Duquesne (Pittsburgh) and routing of the French forces.

During the 1760s this part of western Pennsylvania became a blood-ied land, as a result of an Indian rising led by a chief Pontiac. There were massacres, burnings, lootings, and kidnappings, which resulted years later in the discovery of white children in Indian villages, grown to manhood and womanhood.

While the region was being torn apart by the ravages of the Pontiac rising, Charles Beatty acted as agent for the relief of the poor and dis-tressed and he went on a fund-raising tour of Scotland, England and Wales, returning to Pennsylvania with the princely sum of £4,000.

The McClure-Frisbie missionary partnership in Pittsburgh lasted for most of a year, with both men returning to New England in June, 1773. From then right through the period of the Revolutionary War, the First Pittsburgh Church and the adjoining Long Run congregation were served by young ministerial licentiates of the Donegal Presbytery.

The war meant a large section of the adult population was away from home on the battlefront, and it was the women of the Scots-Irish settlements who kept worship going, largely through prayer meetings for their revolutionary soldier menfolk and, most significantly, for vic-tory over the British.

By 1782, the Redstone Presbytery was formed to embrace the Pittsburgh area and the first clerical members were the Reverends John McMillan, James Power and Thaddens Dodd.

The Scots-Irish Presbyterians of Pittsburgh were among the most gallant on the revolutionary side during the War. The militias led by Aenas Mackey and John Gibson played an important role in the struggle and a young local boy Ebenezer Denny was one of the those chosen to plant the American flag of Independence on the height of the Yorktown battlements.

Forty eight officers in the colonial and revolutionary armies were linked to First Pittsburgh Presbyterian Church, with nearly all of them buried in the church cemetery. They included Irish-born and French-educated General James O'Hara, who had served in the British Coldstream Guards and later became a close associate of George Washington, first as an Indian trader and supplier to the army, and, eventually, as the first quarter-master of the United States.

Interestingly, O'Hara, who married Presbyterian Mary (Polly) Carson, kept a "priest's room" in his home for any travelling clergy and later donated land for the first Roman Catholic Church in the region. He became trustee and was a very generous contributor to First Pittsburgh Church.

The Roman Catholic Church did not receive its first resident priest in Pittsburgh until 1808 and until the beginning of the 19th century First Pittsburgh Presbyterian Church had a monopoly of religion in the city. The first log cabin church for the First Pittsburgh congregation was erected in 1786, with the Pittsburgh Gazette describing it as "a church of squared timbers and moderate dimensions."

German Lutherans and the Episcopal Church did not have an organised presence until the turn of the century. A former Irish Presbyterian minister the Rev John Taylor pioneered Episcopal services in the region.

First Pittsburgh's first minister after the Revolutionary War was the Rev Samuel Barr, described as "a tough little red-haired Ulster-Scot from Londonderry". Educated in Glasgow, Barr was a Calvinist of the old school, who pandered neither to the dictates of political masters or to the religious revivalism that was increasingly prevalent at the time.

Barr, backed by army chaplain Hugh Brackinridge, founded Pittsburgh Academy which later became the Western University of Pennsylvania and, eventually, the University of Pittsburgh.

It was recorded on July 2, 1787 that Pittsburgh had "150 houses and a Presbyterian meeting house with near 400 men". At that time, almost all of the church-going public in the settlement attended the First Pittsburgh one-roomed log cabin church.

While it is acknowledged that under Samuel Barr, First Pittsburgh was never spiritually aggressive, he assiduously taught the children the Bible and Shorter Catechism and his Sunday schools were among the first in the United States. Barr left in 1789 for a new calling in Delaware after successfully facing down a charge from the congregation of failing to live up to his preaching responsibilities.

For 11 years, First Pittsburgh Church was guided by a layman, Scottish-born Judge Alexander Addison, who led most of the residents of the township in resisting the whiskey rebellion against the government. However, a sizeable number of lay members of the Redstone

Presbytery were involved in the Scots-Irish-inspired Whiskey Rebellion of 1794 in western Pennsylvania and they were later refused communion by their ministers and elders until they confessed and repented their sins.

Another Ulsterman, the Rev Robert Steele, from Ballykelly in Co Londonderry, arrived in 1800 with his wife Isabella Hazlett to occupy the First Pittsburgh pulpit. Steele, also theologically educated in Glasgow and ordained at Scriggan near Dungiven by the Derry Presbytery in 1790, had been involved in the aborted 1798 United Irishmen rebellion in Ulster with a number of other Presbyterian ministers and was tried for treason by a court martial.

However, before sentence could be pronounced, he escaped with his wife and baby to America and very probably he was never to know that after leaving Ireland his name was removed from the lists of the Irish synods and presbyteries on the grounds of treason.

Indeed, the Presbytery of Redstone in western Pennsylvania may have been unaware of Steele's turbulent past, having only received a testimonial of his good standing as gospel minister from his previous congregation in Londonderry and some letters of recommendation about his character.

Steele's removal from the roll of the Irish Presbyterian Church is contained in the minutes of the General Synod of Ulster which met in Lurgan on August 28, 1798: "Derry Presbytery report — that Rev Robert Steele, having pleaded guilty to a charge of Treason & Rebellion before a Court Martial, his name was erased from the List of Presbytery".

Described as a very complex man, the scholarly Robert Steele developed a moralistic way of preaching, laying emphasis on correct behaviour and piety. He was a student of the works of William Shakespeare, the great English bard.

By this time a second Presbyterian congregation existed in Pittsburgh, with First in Steele's 10-year ministry generally recognised as the society church and Second the evangelical body, drawn mainly from the small farmers and the lower order tradesmen and their families. In the pews of First Pittsburgh were the military hierarchy and the merchant class and the congregation moved from its log cabin building to a more impressive brick structure.

The Rev Dr Francis Herron, the Pennsylvania-born son of a Covenanting family from Rathfriland in the Mourne Mountain region of Co Down, came to First Pittsburgh in 1811 with the church in a state of crisis.

Materialism, gambling, heavy drinking and profanity had soiled Pittsburgh's image and church-going was in decline. The congregation was heavily in debt due to extravagant building developments and the evangelical Herron set about redressing the situation, both from his prolific organisational and outstanding preaching abilities.

During a 39-year ministry at First Pittsburgh until 1850, Dr Herron made a huge impact, turning around the financial deficit and, most important, enhancing the spiritual vitality of the congregation and in the general social environs of the western Pennsylvania city.

Francis Herron led several significant revivals in the Pittsburgh area and the results of these were manifest in the growth of Sunday schools: by 1833 First Pittsburgh had 12 affiliated Sabbath Schools, with 1,212 scholars and 121 teachers.

During Dr. Herron's ministry, one of the Sunday schools was attended mostly by black children and, throughout the lifetime of the First Pittsburgh congregation there was never any difficulty in accepting people of other races. Africans, Indians and Asiatics have belonged to the church.

The Rev Dr William Millar Paxton, the minister of First Pittsburgh Church from 1851 to 1865, was also of Scots-Irish extraction and a close associate of President Woodrow Wilson, whose grandfather James Wilson came from Strabane in Co Tyrone. Wilson, a Shenandoah Valley man, was president at Princeton College where the theologically brilliant Paxton was a professor.

The Rev Dr George Tybout Purves, acknowledged as one of the greatest pulpit orators of the period in America, was of Scottish ancestry on his father's side, while his mother was a Kennedy from North Antrim. His pastorate at First Pittsburgh covered the period 1886-1892. He left First Pittsburgh to become professor of New Testament at Princeton College and finished his ministry at First Avenue Presbyterian Church in New York

Two other ministers with direct Northern Ireland connections occupied the First Pittsburgh pulpit. One was the Rev Dr Robert J. Lamont, from Philadelphia, whose father James was Ulster-born and a member of the Orange Order back in the Province before emigrating to Pennsylvania to develop his trade as a carpenter. Dr Lamont's mother Marie Rambo was born in Northern Italy and she belonged to the Waldensian Reformed Church of Italy, one of the earliest Protestant denominations.

Lamont was in the highest tradition of preachers in Pittsburgh, serving during the period 1953-73, with attributes which included rugged determination, forthrightness and a pragmatic approach to life. His Scots-Irish business instinct made him one of the great fund-raisers in the American Presbyterian Church of his day and his preaching acumen greatly advanced the spiritual witness at First Pittsburgh.

The present and 14th minister of First Pittsburgh, the Rev Dr Leslie Holmes, was Co Antrim-born and educated in business studies in Belfast before he emigrated at the age of 21 to the United States in 1967 with his wife Barbara. He graduated in theology at Jackson in Mississippi and participated in numerous world ministries, including the US Presbyterian mission to Kenya in East Africa.

Before accepting the call to First Pittsburgh in 1993, Dr Holmes served congregations in Mississippi, Georgia, Florida and California. As a Northern Ireland man born and bred Leslie Holmes is deeply conscious of the important part played by Ulster-Scots immigrants in the formation and growth of the church over 225 years.

The First Pittsburgh congregation has had a long association with the evangelistic crusade of Dr Billy Graham dating back to Dr Lamont's ministry in the 1950s and continuing to the present day. Dr Graham, from Charlotte in North Carolina, is another of Scots-Irish extraction.

The foundation and message of First Pittsburgh Presbyterian Church is: *"Jesus Christ is the same yesterday and today and forever."* (Hebrews chapter 13, verse 8).

12

Ulster settlers *with real character*

The frontier Scots-Irish Presbyterian settlements of western Pennsylvania had a highly distinctive character which even today can still be found in the modern society of Pittsburgh and the surrounding Cumberland Valley region.

Descendants of the early 18th century settlers who moved into western Pennsylvania were dominant community leaders in the region for more than 200 years and Pittsburgh has always been recognised as the strongest Scots-Irish Presbyterian community, for its size, in the United States.

In its commitment to the Presbyterian Calvinist code and an aggressive business enterprise in manufacturing and in merchandising, Pittsburgh has been likened as a city to Belfast, the capital of Northern Ireland.

Pittsburgh, right up until modern times, was a city noted for its Sunday observance and credit for this goes to the Scots-Irish community which dominated life there from the 18th century.

It was said to be a community brought up on "oatmeal and the Ten Commandments". It was also said to be "a compound of worship on Sunday and whiskey on Monday, thus blending the spirits". Pittsburgh had its Methodist, Baptist, Quaker and Roman Catholic communities, but history confirms it was Presbyterianism which took hold of the region from the late 18th century through the 19th century and gave the city its moral fibre.

The first Scots-Irish settlers in the area around Fort Pitt (today Pittsburgh) found their way through the mountainous regions, along passes familiar to the land hunters and fur traders. By 1790, Pittsburgh had become a flourishing town in the midst of a growing region of farmers. Pennsylvania historians confirm the whole territory was prevailingly Scots-Irish, confirmed by the preponderance of Presbyterian churches.

In Pittsburgh it was common to hear the expression: "My family came from the Co Down, or the Co Antrim, or the Co Tyrone". They were a people successful and influential in education, commerce and finance, with three of the largest owners of real estate in Pittsburgh being the Mellons and the Olivers, from Co Tyrone, and the Jones, also from an Ulster strain on the maternal side.

Andrew William Mellon, secretary of the Treasury of the United States, was the son of Judge Thomas A. Mellon, an emigrant from Omagh, Co Tyrone. David B. Oliver, the president of the Pittsburgh board of education, was also Ulster-born, as was United States senator from Western Pennsylvania George T. Oliver, Pennsylvania governor John K. Tener and secretary to the Pennsylvania Commonwealth Robert McAfee.

Thomas A. Mellon was born in 1813 in very humble rural surroundings on a 23-acre farm in the foothills of the Sperrin Mountains in Co Tyrone. He was five-year-old when his father Andrew moved the family to Westmoreland county in western Pennsylvania, and to the then aptly named town of Poverty Point.

Mellon graduated from the Western University of Pennsylvania and he began a successful law practice in Pittsburgh. For 10 years from 1859 he was a judge of the common pleas court of Allegheny county, and in 1870 he established a private banking house in Pittsburgh - T. Mellon and Sons. The firm handled real estate operations and extended substantial credit to men like Andrew Carnegie and Henry C. Frick.

Mellon's great hero was Benjamin Franklin. As a child he read Franklin's autobiography and was deeply impressed by the man. "For one so poor and friendless a boy to be able to become a merchant and a professional man had before seemed an impossibility, but here was Franklin, poorer than myself, who, by industry, thrift and frugality had become learned and wise, and elevated to wealth and fame," wrote

Mellon, who as the son of a small farmer remained a man of the soil with his feet firmly on the ground.

Thomas Mellon married Sarah Jane Negley, a member of one of Pittsburgh's oldest and wealthiest families, and they had eight children (six sons and two daughters), Andrew William being the sixth.

Andrew William Mellon served as secretary of the Treasury from 1920 under three Presidents: Warren G. Harding, Calvin Coolridge and Herbert Hoover, and in 1932 he became American ambassador to Britain. He was one of the most influential figures in the industrial and financial developments of the trans-Allegheny region and was considered the greatest Secretary of the Treasury since Alexander Hamilton, who presided over the nation's finances during the first Presidency of George Washington.

The Mellons were strong Presbyterians with a faith that had been taken across the Atlantic by the emigrant Andrew Mellon. Indeed, Judge Thomas A. Mellon said he brought with him from Ulster, and from his Scots-Irish Presbyterian background "those root principles of right and duty, tenacity of purpose, patient industry and perseverance in well doing which have accompanied me through life."

FIRST CHURCHMEN WEST OF THE ALLEGHENIES

The Rev Charles Beatty, the first Presbyterian minister west of the Allegheny Mountains, was born in Co Antrim in 1715 and pastored in western Pennsylvania from 1758 at the outpost of Fort Pitt (Fort Duquesne), on the site of present-day Pittsburgh.

Beatty was followed by another Scots-Irish cleric the Rev Dr James McMillan, who founded the first school in this section of western Pennsylvania in 1780, and by the Rev Samuel Barr, from Londonderry and another Ulsterman the Rev Robert Steele.

Thomas Dungan, who also came from the north of Ireland, was the first Baptist preacher in Pennsylvania, while the Rev John Black, from Co Antrim, was preaching at the First Reformed Presbyterian (Covenanting) Church in Pittsburgh in 1800. Dr James McMillan founded in his log cabin home in 1787 the Washington Academy, which later became Washington and Jefferson College.

The Scots-Irish influence in the University of Pittsburgh from its inception in 1787 was also very pronounced. By the mid-19th century there were three Presbyterian theological seminaries in western Pennsylvania - Western (started in 1825); Allegheny (1825) and Reformed (1856). The significance of this can be measured by the fact that there were no Roman Catholic theological colleges in western Pennsylvania until 1870.

PRESBYTERIAN CONGREGATIONS IN PENNSYLVANIA, 1698-1730

Meeting House   *Date Established*

1.	New Castle	1698
2.	Philadelphia	1698
3.	Head of Christiana	before 1708
4.	Norriton	1714
5.	Abington	1714
6.	Great Valley	1714
7.	Rock	1720
8.	Lower Brandywine	1720
9.	Lower Octoraro	1720
10.	Upper Octoraro	1720
11.	Donegal	1721
12.	White Clay Creek	1721
13.	Red Clay Creek	1723
14.	Pequea	1724
15.	Nottingham	1725
16.	Neshaminy	before 1926
17.	Deep Run	1726
18.	Middle Octoraro	1727
19.	New London	1728
20.	Derry	1729
21	Paxtang	1729
22.	Faggs Manor	1730
23.	Little Britain	1730
24.	Chestnut Level	1730
25.	Plumstead	1730

13

The *Whiskey rebellion*

The Scots-Irish of western Pennsylvania were largely instrumental in the whiskey insurrection of 1794 against government tariffs imposed on the frontier people. The Scots-Irish were in revolt over taxes levied on whiskey, their principal product and, virtually their only source of income.

The rebellion was a watershed in American politics and one result of the Scots-Irish mutiny was that it motivated federal officials to pay more heed to the needs of those who had settled in the far-flung western frontier territories.

The troubles about the whiskey excise first emerged when Congress adopted the tax in 1791. The Federal Government was badly in need of finance to put the nation's economy in order and so that the debts incurred with the states during the Revolutionary War could be repaid. When the United States Constitution was first adopted the nation's debt was 54 million dollars. Of this sum, 12 million was owed to France and Holland, the while the rest was owed internally.

Alexander Hamilton, the first secretary of the Treasury, pleaded for both the payment of the national debt and the assumption by the Government of the indebtedness which the various states had incurred during the Revolution and which amounted to more than 20 million dollars. To meet the interest on such a vast sum, an annual revenue of 4.5 million dollars was needed and to raise this Congress placed an excise on distilled liquors and a tariff on imported goods.

The whiskey tax alarmed the Scots-Irish farm communities in eastern Pennsylvania and in the western region around Pittsburgh. There, about one in four had a still which produced whiskey (poteen) and other alcoholic substances and the farmers argued that the tax was not only unjust but impossible to meet.

In their situation on the frontier, far removed from the corridors of power in Philadelphia, New York and Boston, whiskey was "not only a commodity, not only a drink, not only a medicine for all ills, not only a source of nourishment, but also a bartering agent in lieu of money."

In the years after the Revolutionary War money was scarce, and the frontiersmen saw very little of it. A farmer of the period recalled that besides his axes he never laid out "more than 10 dollars a year, which was for salt, nails and the like; nothing to wear, eat or drink was purchased, as my farm provided all."

Money may have been in short supply, but whiskey was certainly not and, in western Pennsylvania, rye, from which whiskey was made, grew abundantly. On its own a bushel of rye fetched only 40 cents in 1794, but if it was distilled into whiskey the price soared. A bushel and a half of rye produced a gallon of whiskey and when sold in the eastern cities this fetched a dollar.

Another problem for the frontier farmers was that the payment for the whiskey sales was strictly a paper transaction. Cash was rarely paid out, with contra arrangements between the eastern merchants and the farmers in the purchase of essential goods for life in the western outposts. Without cash the farmers could not pay the excise demanded by Government.

The whiskey rebellion was effectively quelled in 1794, but the ill-feeling over it simmered well into the 19th century with the Scots-Irish settlements in Pennsylvania and in the Appalachian states. The measure was highly unpopular in Virginia, North Carolina, Kentucky and Tennessee and excise officers sent to the frontier to enforce the law were violently treated, with some federal officials publicly humiliated with tarring and feathering.

President George Washington warned those who campaigned against the excise demands "to desist from all unlawful combinations and proceedings whatsoever having for object or tendering to obstruct the operation of the laws." The whiskey rebellion cost the Government

1.5million dollars and 15,000 federal troops sent by President Washington into western Pennsylvania were needed to restore order.

In his book 'The Making of Pennsylvania', Sidney George Fisher wrote: "The western Presbyterians were almost exclusively Scotch-Irish; always sought the frontier and advanced with it westwards. In religion, there was but little difference between the two divisions of Scottish settlers, but in character and temperament the western Scotch-Irish were more excitable and violent".

> *Tell me a tale of the timberlands -*
> *Of the old-time pioneers;*
> *Somepin' a pore man understands*
> *With his feelins 's well as ears.*
> *Tell of the old log house, - about*
> *The loft, and the puncheon flore -*
> *The old fi-er-place, with the crane swung out,*
> *And the latch-string through the door.*
>
> JAMES WHITCOMB RILEY

During the First World War 86 Congressional Medals were awarded for conspicuous bravery on the field of battle. Only 25 of these were given to men who survived, 61 being awarded posthumously. Only one was awarded to those who enlisted from Pennsylvania, to Colonel Joseph H. Thompson of Beaver Falls, Pennsylvania. Colonel Thompson was then major in the 110th Infantry, 28th Division, and he was awarded the medal for conspicuous gallantry and intrepidity above and beyond the call of duty in action near Apremont, France. Joseph H. Thompson was not only Scotch-Irish but Ulster-born.

*"The Scotch-Irishman comes of mighty stock, descending from those
who would fight, who would die, but never surrender. Celt and Saxon
are in him combined, after each has been tempered and refined. As
American citizens the Scotch-Irish have ample reason for pride. They
were the first to proclaim for freedom in these United States; even
before Lexington, Scotch-Irish blood had been shed on behalf of
American freedom. In the forefront of every battle was seen their bur-
nished mail, and in the gloomy retreat was heard their voice of constancy. Next to their intense patriotism, the distinguishing characteristics of the Scotch-Irish are their love of learning and of religion. The
Scotch-Irishman is the ideal educator, and he is a natural theologian.
It would be difficult to find a college or university in America without
a Scotch-Irishman upon its faculty. Another marked characteristic is
the love of home and family, and, wherever this prevails, there are
found mainly virtue, and high integrity, and good citizenship. The
home and the schoolhouse have been mighty forces, marking the
progress of the Scotch-Irish race."*

PRESIDENT WILLIAM McKINLEY (1897-1901),
whose great grandfather came from Conagher near Ballymoney,
Co. Antrim.

14

The harshness of *early frontier life*

The Scots-Irish who settled western Pennsylvania in the 18th century endured great hardships. The journal of the Rev David McClure, written in 1774, records thus:

"The people are mainly Scotch-Irish Presbyterians. On this journey we overtook several families from the older settlements in the east to the west. I remember one in particular, a family of about 12. The man carried a gun and an axe on his shoulders, the wife had the rim of a spinning wheel in one hand and a loaf of bread in the other. The little boys and girls each carried a bundle according to their age. Two poor horses were loaded with some of the bare necessities of life. On top of the baggage of one was a sort of wicker cage in which a baby lay, rocked to sleep by the motion of the horse. A cow was one of the company, and she was destined to bear her part of the family's belongings. A bed cord was strapped around her horns and a bag of meal was on her back. This family was not only patient, but cheerful, pleased at the prospect of finding a happy home in one of the valleys which stretched from the mountains on to Pittsburgh."

The Scots-Irish women, in particular, were a special breed, as the Rev Dr Henry C. McCook, of Philadelphia, pointed out in 1896: "In these humble log huts began the work of home building, constructing that prime factor of all strong and good social order, the family. The family is the unity of society, the true basis of the best civilisation; and in pioneer family building woman was the chief architect.

"The husband indeed must fend and fight for wife and weans, for steading and glebe; he must shoot game, and chop down trees, and clear up fields and plant grain; but the duty and burden of home-making fell upon the wife and mother. And well our pioneer Scotch-Irish pioneers did their work. What sort of plenishing had these frontier heroines for their new cabin homes?

"There was neither bedstead nor stool nor chair not bucket; no domestic comfort, but such as could be carried on pack horses through the wilderness. Two rough boxes, one on the other, served as a table; two kegs for seats, and so on. Having committed themselves to God in family worship they spread their bed on the floor and slept soundly until morning. Sometimes, indeed, they had no bread for weeks together; but had plenty of pumpkins and potatoes, and all the necessities of life. Pumpkins and potatoes! Necessities of life!

"The original settlers, of course, did not even have the luxuries of pumpkins and potatoes, to begin their culinary duties therewith. They had, in sooth, to invent a cuisine. Everything must be found anew. The wild fruits, wild berries and wild game and the fish of the New World were utilised. Indian corn was a new cereal to these Ulster housewives: but it had to be wrought into the primitive menu, mush and milk!

"It was a novel sort of porridge for our grandams, but they learned to make it. Cooking was not the only sphere that solicited her creative faculty. The pioneer woman had to invent a pharmacopoeia. Wounds and sickness came, and must be cared for. The forest was full of healing herbs - and perhaps our octogenarian members still have recollections of ginseng and snakeroot teas, and slippery elm poultices, and the like.

"The women pioneer had to be physician and surgeon, trained in nurse and apothecary, all in one, and often supplied the patient, too, in her own person. In times of personal sickness and during the illness of children, the strain upon women thus situated must have been intense. Such a life indeed developed self-reliance; fertility of resources, strong and independent characters; but many fell under the grievous strain, and thus became veritable martyrs of civilisation."

The Scots-Irish, like the German settlers, had large families and it required the continued toil of the wife and mother to ensure that everyone had warm clothing. In their one-room log cabin homes, the women did the weaving and spinning of the wool and yarn for all the cloth worn by the family.

Deerskin and leather breeches were generally worn by the men and the boys, although on occasions the women and girls had to use the same materials.

It was said that the conduct of the Scots-Irish frontier inhabitant demonstrated their faith, their patriotism and their spirit of mutual helpfulness. The early pioneer was not a philosopher and a thinker in the academic sense. In the rigorous struggle for survival in a virtual wilderness, there was not the time to develop these interests. In the early 18th century, the average frontiersman was a doer whose values and beliefs were reflected in his everyday behaviour.

The Scots-Irish frontiersman has been described elsewhere as "a type of man who was high-principled and narrow, strong and violent, as tenacious of his own rights as he was blinded often to the rights of others; acquisitive yet self-sacrificing, but most of all fearless, confident of his own power, determined to have and to hold."

Distinguished 19th century American statesman Henry Cabot Lodge classified the Scots-Irish as a distinctive race stock. He said: "I classified the Scotch-Irish and the Irish as two distinctive race stocks and I believe the distinction is a sound one, both historically and scientifically.

"The Scotch-Irish from the north of Ireland, Protestant in religion, and chiefly Scotch and English in blood and name, came to this country in large numbers in the 18th century; while the people of pure Irish stock came scarcely at all during the colonial period and did not emigrate here largely until the present century was well advanced."

* A 1790 census of almost 3,000 white families in western Pennsylvania's five counties (Allegheny, Washington, Fayette, Westmoreland and Bedford) used the surnames of the heads of families to distinguish their ethnic origin. Such a method was hardly the most accurate in a census, but the findings are interesting: English 37 per cent, Scottish 17, German 12, Ulster Scottish 7.5, Welsh 7, Anglo-Irish 4.6, Irish Celtic 4.6, Ulster Celtic 2.7, others 8. The Scots-Irish were strongest in Allegheny county, where they constituted 25 per cent.

The 1790 census reveals that in no American state did the Scots-

Irish population rival the English, but in every state except New York and Pennsylvania it stood second. The percentage of Scots-Irish in Pennsylvania in 1790 was 19.6. The average Scots-Irish family then consisted of 5.67 members, compared with 5.77 for the English.

The extent of the movement of the Scots-Irish from Pennsylvania through the Shenandoah Valley to the more western regions through the 18th century were such that the Great Wagon Road from Pennsylvania. along which they ventured by wagon, horseback or on foot, was commonly referred to as "the Irish Road".

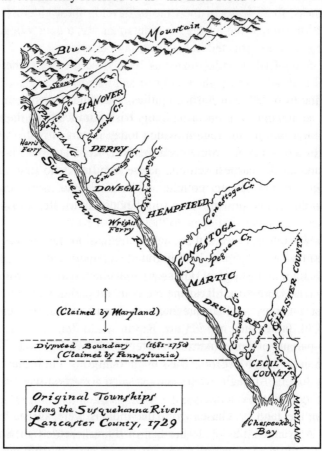

Original Townships along the Susquehanna River
Lancaster County, 1729

15

Ulster families *in the Kishacoquillas*

The lush valley of Kishacoquillas in middle Pennsylvania was a settlement for pioneering Scots-Irish families from the summer of 1766. In this region, which today is part of Mifflin County, the Alexander, Brown, McDowell, McNitt, Reed and Taylor families were among the earliest settlers. These families, who first settled in Cumberland and Chester counties of Pennsylvania, were acquainted back in Ulster and on American soil they continued the relationship.

James Alexander first came to the valley of Kishacoquillas in 1754, but he was twice driven out by Indian aggression. James was born in Co. Armagh in 1726 and he emigrated to America in 1736 with his parents John and Margaret (Glasson) Alexander and two brothers and two sisters. He married Rosanna Reed in 1762 and they had 11 children, seven sons and four daughters, all born between the years 1763 and 1786. James died in 1791 and Rosanna in 1792.

The parents of James Alexander were both Scottish born – John in Lanarkshire and Margaret Glasson in Glasgow. They married and moved to Co. Armagh, where they resided for upwards of a decade before the trek to America.

After the land purchases from the Indians were agreed in 1754, Hugh Alexander, the elder brother of James, settled in Shermans Valley, while James pushed further west to the valley of Kishacoquillas, which was attractive for the excellence of its soil, valuable timber and fine springs. James located and received a tract of 239 acres, but after erecting a log cabin he was driven out in 1756 when Indian tribes were raiding this section of the country. This was at the height of the French/Indian War and the white settlers faced grave dangers in the pioneering frontier regions.

About 1762, when the trouble with the Indians had subsided, James Alexander and his wife Rosey (Rosanna) returned to Kishacoquillas and a log house, with a capacious fireplace, was erected to replace the original log cabin. This was later replaced by a stone house.

By 1773 James had acquired a further 180 acres of land, by 1786 150 acres and by 1793 200 acres to leave him with an estate of upwards of 1,000 acres. During the Revolutionary War he served in the commissionary department of George Washington's army at Valley Forge during the winter of 1777-78 and for this service he obtained 1,600 acres at Clearfield county, Pennsylvania.

James was founder and ruling elder of West Kishacoquillas Presbyterian Church and he is buried in the churchyard. His lands were divided up among his family who married into Scots-Irish kinsfolk in the area. During his residence in the Kishacoquillas Valley, James Alexander created the township of Armagh, in memory and honour of his homeland back in Ulster. Some descendants of James and Rosanna Alexander moved to Kentucky, Tennessee, Arkansas and Illinois, but most stayed in Pennsylvania and the family link is still strong in the Valley of Kishacoquillas.

Hugh Alexander, a brother of James, was a member of the Council of Deputies and of the first Presbyterian assembly, which met in Carpenters Hall, Philadelphia on November 28, 1776. John, another brother, also served in the revolutionary army.

Two cousins – Hugh and James Alexander – travelled with the family from the north of Ireland, to America, but they set up home at Mecklenburg county in North Carolina.

The house which James Alexander built was a fort-like structure of huge oak logs, dressed down from either side to a uniform thickness of seven and one half inches, some of them 20 inches across the face, and securely locked together at the corners with sloping dove-tail joints, which effectively shed the water. Despite the great size and weight of the timbers, this work was as accurate as though it had been built by a cabinetmaker.

The journal of Presbyterian minister the Rev. Charles Beatty, who travelled the region in 1766, contains an illuminating reference to the Kishacoquillas settlement: "There is another settlement just begun, consisting of six or seven families, four miles from the former (settlement), over a mountain, called Kithaquaquilla or Great Valley, extending about 30 miles and five or six wide. As the land there is very good, a greater number of people is expected to settle there in the Spring."

Since the term "settlement" refers to the entire valley, it would appear that not many settlers were actually upon the ground that year.

William Brown and James Reed settled near James Alexander's homestead in 1755 and tradition says they were half-brothers. William was an early justice of the peace in Kishacoquillas Valley and he owned a gristmill. In the Revolutionary War, William served as a commissionary in George Washington's army and in 1789 he became one of the first judges in Mifflin county. James Reed also became a leading citizen in Kishacoquillas Valley, as a farmer, militiaman and Presbyterian.

John McDowell, of Co. Antrim stock, settled in the valley in 1761 and was a revolutionary soldier and a community leader in the Antrim township. He and a sister-in-law of James Alexander, had 13 children.

The McNitts, Alexander and William, were first settled in Kishacoquillas valley in 1770, followed by brothers John, Robert and James. They were sons of Ulster-born Robert McNitt (also written in historical records as McNut and McKnitt), who lived in Lurgan township, now Franklin county, Pennsylvania until 1765.

Armagh township embraced the whole of the Kishacoquillas valley from its establishment in 1770 to 1790. It had earlier been a part of Derry township, and before that of Fermanagh township. In 1790 Armagh township was broken up with Union the new name of settlements to the west.

Scots-Irish families who lived there were Armstrong, Alexander, Allen, Allison, Ashcroft, Barr, Bell, Brown, Campbell, Emmett, Fleming, Gardner, Houston, Hazlett, Kenney, Kyle, Lyon, Logan, McDowell, McClelland, McElroy, McClenaghan, Mateer, McNamara, McIntire, McCalla, Nelson, Riddle, Reed, Stewart, Sample, Sankey, Scott, Tanyer, Vance, Wilson, Young and Wills.

Two of the Alexander land warrants in Kishacoquillas county are of special interest because of the focus they throw upon the period when the first settlements in this region were actually made, and upon the manner in which the settlers established themselves upon their land. They are dated February 5, 1755, the second day after the opening of the Land Office for granting warrants upon land west of the Susquehanna. One was issued in the name of James Alexander, and the other for his brother, John Alexander Jr., both of whom are described as "of Cumberland County," though in other documents their place of origin is given as West Nottingham Township, Chester county. These warrants confirm that the two brothers had taken possession of their land, built a log cabin, and planted their first crop of wheat in the summer and fall of 1754.

WARRANT NO.26 – BY THE PROPRIETARIES

"Whereas James Alexander of the county of Cumberland hath requested that we would grant him to take up one hundred acres of land on the Eastern branch of a Run near the North Mountain including his cabin in Kishycoquillis Valley, County of Cumberland, for which he agrees to pay to our use, fifteen pounds, ten shillings, current money of this province, for said hundred acres, and the yearly Quit-Rent of one half-penny sterling for every acre thereof.

"These are therefore to authorise and require you to survey or cause to be surveyed unto the said James Alexander, at the place aforesaid, according to the method of townships appointed, the said quantity of one hundred acres, if not already surveyed or appropriated, and make return thereof into the secretary's office, in order for further confirmation; for which this shall be your sufficient warrant: which survey, in case the said James Alexander fulfil the above agreement within six months from the date thereof, shall be valid, otherwise void. Given under my hand and seal of the land office, by virtue of certain powers from the said proprietaries at Philadelphia, this fifth day of February Anno Domini One Thousand Seven Hundred and Fifty Five."

ROBT. H. MORRIS.
To Nicholas Scull, Surveyor General.

The warrant to John Alexander Jr., was couched in similar terms, "Whereas John Alexander Jun'r of the County of Cumberland hath requested that we would grant him to take up fifty acres of land near the North Mountain near the Head of the South Branch of Kishycoquillis, including a wheat patch, in the said County of Cumberland, etc."

The early warrants were necessarily vague about the location of the land to be taken up, being orders of survey upon a region never before surveyed. It was for this reason that outstanding features of the land were sometimes mentioned as means of identification. In this case, James Alexander's tract was to be recognised by "his cabin", and that of his brother by "a wheat patch".

The latter indication is particularly significant: for as a "wheat patch" in February must have been sown in the preceding Fall, upon land previously cleared of its virgin growth, and reduced to a state of cultivation, it is established that the initial work of settlement and improvement was begun not later than the summer of 1754. The log cabin, no doubt, was erected at the same time. This is the only proven instance, so far as the historians have discovered, of a bona fide settlement of land in the Kishacoquillas Valley before the year 1755.

The Alexander brothers were not alone in making so early an entry of their land. Twenty warrants are recorded for the Kishacoquillas Valley in 1755, and it can be assumed that some at least of the other warrantees began their improvements at the same time.

It should be remembered, however, that the mere existence of a warrant was no proof of an actual settlement; for in a number of cases warrants were issued to those who never came to the valley, or who, if they did come, failed to make it their home.

Robert Fulton, the man who first applied steam to water navigation, was born in Lancaster county, Pennsylvania, of Scots-Irish parents who emigrated from Ulster around 1730. His father was a founder of the Presbyterian Church at Lancaster.

Letter to the *Yankee Club*

LETTER TO THE YANKEE CLUB OF STEWARTSTOWN, IN THE COUNTY OF TYRONE, AND PROVINCE OF ULSTER, IRELAND.

Gentlemen, it is with unfeigned satisfaction I accept your congratulations on the late happy and glorious revolution. The generous indignation, against the foes to the rights of human nature, with which you seem so animated, and the exalted sentiments or liberty, which you appear to entertain; are too consonant to the feelings and principles of the citizens of the United States of America, not to attract their veneration and esteem; did not the affectionate and anxious concern with which you regarded their struggle for freedom and independence, entitle you to their more particular acknowledgements. If, in the course of our successful contest, any good consequence have resulted to the oppressed kingdom of Ireland, it will afford a new source of felicitation to all who respect the interests of humanity. I am now, gentlemen, to offer you my best thanks for the indulgent sentiments you are pleased to express of my conduct; and for your benevolent wishes respecting my personal welfare, as well as with regard to a more interesting object – the prosperity of my country. I have the honour to be, with due consideration, gentlemen, your most obedient, humble servant.

GEORGE WASHINGTON,
Mount Vernon, Virginia, January 20, 1784.

George Washington it was who said, *"If defeated everywhere else, I will make my last stand for liberty amongst the Scots-Irish of my native Virginia."*

16

Ulster-born Quakers
who settled in Pennsylvania

James Logan, the governor of Pennsylvania during the early 18th century, was an Ulsterman born and bred, but unlike most of his fellow countrymen who emigrated to America he was a Quaker and was far removed from some of the quirkier characteristics of the Presbyterians.

This colonial visionary who was appointed secretary to William Penn after they had engaged in shipping transactions between Bristol and Dublin was born in Lurgan, Co. Armagh in 1674, the son of an Anglican clergyman, Patrick Logan, who later became a Quaker. Patrick Logan moved to Lurgan to take charge of a Latin school and James was born at High Street in the town.

At the age of 13, James was apprenticed to a Dublin linen merchant Edward Webb, but, because of the unsettled state of Ireland at the time, he rejoined the family in Lurgan after a stay of only six months and they all returned to Scotland, where Patrick Logan was born and educated at Edinburgh University.

By 1690, the Logans had moved to Bristol with Patrick appointed master of a Quaker school. Three years later he and his family moved back to Lurgan, leaving James at the age of 19 in charge of the school. Teaching prepared James for the entry into business enterprises in Bristol which involved shipping interests with Dublin.

William Penn, a governor in the Bristol school, was impressed by Logan's abilities and he took James with him to America in 1699 as his secretary. Over the next 40 years, James Logan held various high offices, including governor of Pennsylvania, mayor of Philadelphia and chief judge of the supreme court in the colony.

Logan was devoted to his the interests of the Penn family and the liberal Quaker ideals, which led to the foundation of Pennsylvania. He was a skilled negotiator and earned the respect of the Indian tribes during the land dealings. His scholarly activities were formidable and he amassed a considerable library. He died in 1751.

William Penn was the son of Admiral Penn who was granted a province in America by King Charles II in return for service on behalf of the Monarchy. The Admiral left the colonising to his son and after William visited the Rhineland area in mainland Europe, known as the Palatinate, he befriended local Lutheran groups and encouraged them to settle the lands inherited by him along the banks of the Delaware River.

The Penn family retained the land until it was purchased by the Commonwealth of Pennsylvania in 1776 and the earliest permanent settlers were the Scots-Irish Presbyterians, Swiss and German Mennonites, German Lutherans, French Huguenots, English Quakers and Welsh Episcopalians.

The Scots-Irish and the French Huguenots sought out the earliest frontier of Pennsylvania by settling to the south-west and western extremes where they traded with the indians of the Chesapeake Bay region, and west of the Allegheny Mountains and into the Ohio and Mississippi Valleys.

James Logan was responsible for the colonisation of the Pennsylvania province in the early 18th century with thousands of Ulster-Scots Presbyterians. At first he was enthusiastic about the prospects for the Ulster settlers, but the buoyancy turned to concern when the immigrants virtually over-ran the lands.

Logan wrote in 1729: "It looks as if Ireland is to send all its inhabitants hither, for last week not less than six ships arrived and every day two or three arrive also. The common fear is that if they continue they will make themselves proprietors of the province. The Indians are alarmed at the swarms of strangers, and we are afraid of a breach between them, for the Irish are very rough to them".

This reaction from Logan was in sharp contrast to his original invite to the first group of Ulster-Scots families ("brave fellow countrymen") to settle in the colony. He wrote in 1720: "At the time we were apprehensive from the Northern Indians. I therefore thought it might be prudent to plant a settlement of such men who formerly had so bravely defended Londonderry and Inniskillen as a frontier in case of any disturbance. These people if kindly used will be orderly as they have hitherto been and easily dealt with. They will also, I believe, be a leading example to others".

The first Ulster settlers in Pennsylvania were given lands at Chester County, now Lancaster County, and the settlement was known as Donegal. Within a few years, Logan had become so disenchanted with the Scots-Irish settlers that he was calling them "bold and indigent strangers". Their failure to properly recognise land titles and the tendency to squat on other people's land vexed him greatly.

Logan held to the view that "a settlement of five families from the north of Ireland gives me more trouble than fifty of other people. They are troublesome settlers to the government and hard neighbours to the Indians".

From 1729, James Logan was refusing to issue land rights to the Scots-Irish families. The Penn family were disturbed by developments and they wrote to Logan recommending that the Pennsylvania assembly pass a law prohibiting further emigration by both the Scots-Irish and the German Palatine Protestants. But the flood of people was by then too great to halt as the settlements took root and the Scots-Irish placed themselves in positions of influence.

The Scots-Irish people who settled in America in the 18th century were a progressive community and it is interesting to acknowledge their main interests of achievement alongside the German Palatinate Lutherans who were on the frontier at the same time. Scots-Irish excelled in education, government, law, the stage, invention and the military, while the Germans were best at art, music, science, philanthropy and business.

Prepared to sell themselves *into service*

An advertisement in the Belfast News Letter of March 6, 1738 shows that even at that early date Ulster-Scots were prepared to sell themselves into service in order to reach the new American country.

It reads: "This is to give notice, that the snow (ship) Charming Molly, Mr. Henry McLachlan, master, will be well fitted out, manned and victualled, and clear to sail from Belfast to New-Castle or Pennsylvania in America, against the first day of May next, the said Mr. McLachlan will trade with any who have goods to transport thither, or go as passengers redemptions, or servants, on the most easy and reasonable terms".

A larger advertisement in the Belfast News Letter of October 31, 1769 shows that the same practice prevailed of immigrants selling their services in advance and going out to the new country as "redemptioners".

"The young men of Ireland who wish to be free and happy should leave it and come here as quickly as possible. There is no place in the world where a man meets so rich a reward for good conduct and industry as in America."

- Contents of a letter from John Dunlap to Robert Rutherford in Ulster. Dated May 12, 1785. John Dunlap, originally from Strabane in Co. Tyrone, was the official printer of the Declaration of Independence in 1776.

17

Scots-Irish families *of Pennsylvania*

THE DICKS

This family can trace back to William Dick, who was born near Belfast and in the late 18th century emigrated to Pennsylvania, where he married Anna McGunnegle, the daughter of a strong Scots-Irish family. Few men or families on the American frontier have been so thoroughly identified with the building up of the region as the Dicks of western Pennsylvania.

William Dick settled in the Pittsburgh region and with his five sons left an indelible mark on frontier society there. His second son John became a militia general, merchant, banker, justice and politician, making it to Congress as a Republican, but still operating from his base at Meadville, Pennsylvania. He was an unsuccessful Vice-Presidential candidate in 1856 when John C. Fremont took on James Buchanan.

John's son Samuel Bernard Dick followed his father into mercantile affairs and was a successful banker in Meadville city. However, he became a soldier when the Civil War broke out in 1861 and was a captain of the Ninth Pennsylvania Regiment, a force that saw battle at Drainsville, Richmond and Bull Run. He was very seriously wounded and hostilities took a toll of his health, but he returned later in the War to lead the 56th Pennsylvania Regiment into Virginia.

He had come of a long line of soldiers, from the Revolutionary War to the Civil War. George Dick, his father's brother, was killed in the

Patriot War in Texas, and his own brother George, a Confederate, died in the army just before the Civil War, having been the adjutant of General Robert E. Lee's regiment.

After the war, Samuel Bernard Dick became a Congressman and continued in business at Meadville. He was for a time Grand Master of the Masonic Order in Pennsylvania.

THE MACFARLANES

John J. MacFarlane, a Pennsylvania state senator from 1882 and president of the American life Insurance Company of Philadelphia, was the son of an Ulster-born couple who emigrated in the early 19th century. He was a successful businessman and politician who stuck to the old Scots-Irish maxim of "he who best helps himself, most helps the world."

THE BARRS

Distinguished 19th century Pittsburgh journalist and publisher James P. Barr was the grandson of an Ulster couple who moved to Greensburg, Pennsylvania with their four children about 1799. His father Daniel H. Barr was an ardent follower of Thomas Jefferson and Andrew Jackson and he fought in the War of 1812. He was a justice of the peace, postmaster and state collector for the Pennsylvanian canal.

James P. Barr worked with several newspapers before becoming editor and principal proprietor of the Pittsburgh Post. He vigorously championed the cause of Democratic candidate Stephen A. Douglas in the 1860 Presidential election which Abraham Lincoln won. He served three years as surveyor-general for Pennsylvania.

THE CRAWFORDS

General Samuel Wylie Crawford, a Union Army hero of Gettysburg, was of Covenanting Presbyterian stock who arrived at Charleston, South Carolina from the north of Ireland.

The family were originally lowland Scots from Ayrshire and Renfrewshire and it was Nathan Crawford and his wife Margaret

Wylie who crossed the Atlantic with other Ulster families in the early 1770s. They lived at Fisher's Creek at Chester county in the Carolina Piedmont region until 1794 when yellow fever tragically caused their deaths and left a boy and a girl orphans.

The children were taken to Pennsylvania and the son Samuel Wylie Crawford became a Covenanting Presbyterian minister, witnessing for the faith for many years at Conecocheague Creek and holding the principalship of the Academical Department at the University of Pennsylvania. An uncle the Rev Samuel V. Wylie was vice-provost of the University and professor of languages for many years.

Samuel Wylie Jun., the soldier, was born at Conecocheague Creek and he received a classical education at the University of Pennsylvania. His army career took him to Texas in 1851 and for three years he served at various forts, including El Paso.

In the Civil War he fought at Fort Sumter, Winchester, Cedar Mountain and South Mountain and Gettysburg and was engaged in the Potomac army engagements.

After the war, he travelled extensively in Britain, Europe and the Middle East, receiving the attentions of government, military and social leaders, who, it was said, took stock of his reputation and military advice.

THE ADAMS'S

Robert Adams, of Lifford Hall on the Tyrone/Donegal border in Ulster, emigrated to America in 1793 and within a few years he had established himself as a successful merchant in the Philadelphia area. A grandson, another Robert Adams, was a leading Pennsylvanian state senator for the Republican Party in the latter part of the 19th century.

THE KELLEYS

The ancestors of 19th century Pennsylvania lawyer and statesman William Darrah Kelley were among the earliest settlers of West Jersey in a small colony of Ulster Presbyterians and French Huguenot Protestants. Both the Kelleys and Darrahs, his mother's family, eventually moved to Philadelphia.

William Darrah Kelley, born in 1814, emerged as a Philadelphia judge and, although he initially sided with the Democratic Party, he was influenced by the politics of Abraham Lincoln and in 1860 was elected to the US Congress, where he served for 22 years.

THE PATTONS

Colonel John Patton, from Sligo in the north west of Ireland, emigrated in 1761 and was a prosperous merchant in Philadelphia. During the Revolutionary War, Patton served as colonel of the 16th Regiment, Pennsylvania line and had charge of the defences of Philadelphia during a critical time in the war.

Patton was one of a number of patriotic merchants who raised, on their own private bond, £260,000 to aid George Washington in his cause. When he died in 1804 he was major-general of a division state militia. A grandson John Patton succeeded as central Pennsylvania merchant and banker and was a US Congressman.

THE HOUSTONS

John Houston and his wife and six children came from Co Antrim in 1730 and located at Carlisle township in Pennsylvania. After a few years, they were driven out by an Indian uprising and moved to 1,000 acres at Pequa Valley in Lancaster county.

The Pennsylvania Houstons are thought to be kinsfolk of the descendants of General Sam Houston of Tennessee and Texas and they had distinguished service in the Revolutionary War, with John's grandson James dying from wounds received at the Battle of Paoli. A brother, Glasgow-educated Dr John Houston, was a surgeon in the revolutionary army and one of the pioneer physicians of York county, Pennsylvania.

18

Prominent *Scots-Irish Pennsylvanians*

- **CHARLES THOMSON**, born in Maghera in Co. Londonderry, was the man who designed the Great Seal of America and was the secretary of the American Continental Congress for 15 years from 1774. When the new federal constitution was adopted in 1789, Thomson was delegated to convey to George Washington at his Mount Vernon home in Virginia the request of Congress that he become the first President. The original Declaration of Independence of July 4, 1776 bore only two signatures, that of John Hancock, President of Congress and, Charles Thomson.

  Thomson was born at Gorteade, Upperlands near Maghera in 1729 and the family belonged to Maghera Presbyterian Church. When his mother died, Charles emigrated to America as a 10-year-old with his father John and five brothers and sister. Tragically, his father took ill and died as their ship entered Delaware Bay and the children were orphans on arrival on American soil.

  Charles had a brief apprenticeship as a blacksmith, but through sponsorship from a kindly and wealthy lady he received a classical education in Pennsylvania and graduated as a teacher in Greek and Latin at Philadelphia Academy, the forerunner of the University of Philadelphia. He later moved into the mercantile business, before espousing the politics of the Whig movement and he became a contemporary of Benjamin Franklin, Thomas Jefferson and John Adams.

Thomson designed the Great Seal of America in 1782 and, in his role as secretary to the Continental Congress, he was known as "the venerable patriot". In retirement, Charles Thomson spent most of his time translating the Old and New Testaments of the Bible into the Greek Septuagint version. He died in 1824, aged 95.

• **THOMAS COCHRAN**, son of Scots-Irish couple Robert B. and Mary Allison Cochran, was a Philadelphia lawyer from 1854 and a member of the Pennsylvania house of representatives. After the financial demands of the Civil War, he and two associates on a judicial board succeeded in preventing the city of Philadelphia from going bankrupt. He was acknowledged as one of leading financiers of his day.

• **JAMES DUNCAN**, soldier, merchant and public official in Philadelphia, was of Scots-Irish stock and very early in the Revolutionary War he was commissioned as a lieutenant after having second thoughts about a career as a Presbyterian minister.

The Princeton-educated Duncan fought in the various battles on American and Canadian soil leading up to the success over the British at Yorktown and when the War was over he returned to develop business interests in Philadelphia and develop his Presbyterian church interests.

Duncan owned a store at Abbotstown, York county, Pennsylvania and for several years he held the lucrative contract to supply provisions to the garrison at Carlisle barracks. For ten pence each - and Duncan specifically wanted English pence rather than American cents - he sold rations of beef, pork, bread or flour and whiskey. And it is recorded that for every hundred rations sold, he added supplies of soap, candles, vinegar and salt. He was an entrepreneur in the best Scots-Irish tradition. Duncan became a close Republican Party associate of Governor Thomas McKean, who was also of Scots-Irish vintage, and fought several elections to Congress.

• **DANIEL HARTMAN HASTINGS**, whose father was born in Ireland and mother in Scotland, was adjutant-general of Pennsylvania in the late 1880s and was a leading academic, lawyer and journalist in the state. Self-taught, Daniel Hartman Hastings worked on the family farm at Clinton county until he was14, but he made it to the bar and fought in the Civil War for the Federal cause.

- **THOMAS McCAMANT**, another adjutant-general of Pennsylvania, was widely considered to be one of the strong men of the state during the late 19th century. His great-great grandfather Alexander McCamant emigrated from Ulster in 1733, settling in both Philadelphia and Lancaster county after buying land from the Penn family. The McCamants were among the pioneers of Presbyterianism in the central region of Pennsylvania and Thomas McCamant was acknowledged as a mover and shaker in Republican politics.

- **JUSTICE JOSEPH BREWSTER McCOLLUM**, a member of the Supreme Court of Pennsylvania for several decades until the late 1880s, was of Scots-Irish farming stock from the eastern Susquehanna region. McCollum was both a journalist and lawyer who propagated the Democratic cause.

- **SILAS MOORHEAD CLARK**, justice of the Supreme Court of Pennsylvania, is descended from a Scots-Irish family which first settled in the Cumberland Valley in the early 18th century and moved to western Pennsylvania to engage in iron manufacturing. A maternal forebear Fergus Moorhead was held captive by Indians in July, 1776, taken to Quebec and sold to the British. After a year of imprisonment he rejoined his family, travelling on foot from New York to his home in the Cumberland Valley. Judge Clark, a Democrat, had a long and distinguished career at the bar and was elected to the Supreme Bench in 1882.

- **CHARLES WILLIAM MACKEY**, Civil War soldier, lawyer, businessman and politician, was the grandson of a Scot from Inverness and an Ulsterwoman from Co Tyrone. The family settled in Chester county and were prominent in Presbyterian church circles and the Democratic Party. Charles William Mackey was a leading attorney for the major railroad companies in the United States and was heavily involved in banking.

- **ROBERT MURPHY**, born in Co Antrim in 1776, became one of Philadelphia's most generous philanthropists after arriving in the city in 1796. He was a shoe manufacturer, and worked for a time as a tax collector. He was noted for his benevolence, meeting the ships from Ireland at the wharf and giving money and provisions to the needy.

  Murphy often conducted services in charitable institutions and, although originally a Presbyterian, he was a member of the St Paul's Methodist Episcopal Church in Philadelphia.

- **GEORGE WILLIAM MILLER** was one of the most prominent members of the Democratic Party in the second half of the 19th century, with the Ulster connection traced to his grandfather who was one of the founders of Jefferson College at Canonsburg. Miller was a Washington lawyer and he was appointed marshal of the western district of Pennsylvania by President Grover Cleveland.

- **HUGH M. NORTH**, the Chief Justice of the United States Court of Claims, was a member of a Scots-Irish family from Juniata county, Pennsylvania. His grandfather on his mother's side Hugh McAllister was one of the earliest settlers in that county and a Revolutionary War major. Hugh M. North, a Democrat, served in the Pennsylvania house of representatives from 1854.

- **MAXWELL STEVENSON**, prominent at the bar and in Philadelphia politics as a Democrat, was born in Co Tyrone in 1847 and emigrated to America with his family when only four. Stevenson was said to have inherited all the obdurate, uncompromising and native shrewdness of Scots-Irish Presbyterianism

- **THOMAS JAMISON STEWART**, the Secretary of Internal Affairs in Pennsylvania, was born outside Belfast in 1848 and emigrated to America with his parents as an infant. He fought in the Civil War with the 38th Pennsylvania Regiment and served as a Republican member of the state legislature.

The scene in Pittsburgh, Pennsylvania in 1762 as the Scots-Irish settlers were arriving.

The present-day exterior and interior of the Donegal Presbyterian Church at Elizabethtown in eastern Pennsylvania.

The 18th century James Fulton homestead at Elizabethtown in eastern Pennsylvania, which has now been moved to the Ulster-American Folk Park at Omagh, Co Tyrone.

President James Buchanan and his first lady and niece Harriet Lane.

The 18th century Scots-Irish pioneering families carve a pathway through the Appalachian forests and mountains.

*First Pittsburgh Presbyterian Church: the log cabin church of 1787
and the more imposing churches of 1805 and 1853 (right).*

Early Ulster-born ministers of First Pittsburgh Presbyterian Church

Rev Charles Beatty

Rev Samuel Barr

Rev Robert Steele

Rev Francis Herron

An engraving of Daniel Boone based on the painting
by Warren Chappel (1820-1885). New York Public Picture Collection.

General Benjamin Logan, 18th century Kentuckian and son of Ulster-born settlers.

General George Rogers Clark, another Ulster-Scot, Virginian militiaman and early Kentucky pioneer.

The Sunday School chapel of First Pittsburgh Presbyterian Church 1881.

*American country music performers from Kentucky with Scots-Irish roots:
the late Bill Monroe and Ricky Skaggs.*

A typical 18th century rural Pennsylvania settlement
by Scots-Irish families.

Londonderry, Northern Ireland's second city.

The County Antrim coast road.

CITY OF PHILADELPHIA

Welcome

Whereas...

Billy Kennedy, the internationally acclaimed author of three Scotch-Irish books - best sellers in both Britain and the United States - will visit Philadelphia on Saturday, March 14, 1998. Billy Kennedy is also the assistant editor of the Belfast News Letter, Northern Ireland's leading morning newspaper, which was founded in 1737 and carried the European exclusive story in 1776 of the signing of the American Declaration of Independence.

Kennedy, who has traveled extensively throughout the United States in his research of Scotch-Irish history is preparing his fourth book. It will encompass the states of Pennsylvania, Kentucky, Georgia, West Virginia, Missouri, Mississippi and Texas. He is appealing to families with direct links to the early Scotch-Irish settlers in those states to contact him as he is keen to trace their genealogy for possible inclusion in the book.

Now, Therefore...

I, Edward G. Rendell, Mayor of the City of Philadelphia, do hereby extend a warm and cordial welcome to

BILLY KENNEDY

and urge all Philadelphians, especially those of Scotch-Irish descent, to applaud this man's accomplishments and warmly receive him in our City of Brotherly Love.

Edward G. Rendell

MAYOR

Given under my hand and the Seal of the City of Philadelphia, this fourteenth day of March, one thousand, nine hundred and ninety-eight.

Welcome from Philadelphia, city of Brotherly Love.

19

The Hamiltons *of Juniata River*

John Hamilton of Fermanagh was the self-proclaimed title of a second generation Ulsterman who settled on the Juniata River in central Pennsylvania in the 1760s. John, who took this title to differentiate himself from other John Hamiltons in the region, was an entrepreneur of some standing, owning a general store, a mill, and considerable land holdings at his Fermanagh settlement.

His father John arrived in Pennsylvania from Coleraine in 1741 and tragically his wife Isabella Potter died upon arriving on American soil. John Sen. married a second time, Jane Allen, of wealthy English stock, and John of Fermanagh was a son of this marriage.

John of Fermanagh served in several campaigns of the Revolutionary War as a militia captain and he and his men marched to Trenton, arriving the day after George Washington's army defeated the Hessians in the battle there.

The Fermanagh home was a fieldstone mansion and John married Margaret Alexander, daughter of Hugh Alexander who signed the 1776 constitution of Pennsylvania in Philadelphia. Expanding his territory, John of Fermanagh purchased land beside the Susquehanna River from Yorkshireman John Harris and he erected the first brick residence in the newly founded Harrisburg, a city which later became, and still is the capital of Pennsylvania.

John's son Hugh was a Harrisburg lawyer who married Rosanna Boyd, daughter of Scotsman Adam Boyd, and later he went into the newspaper publishing and printing business. He was a close associate of President James Buchanan, who was also of Ulster stock, and was followed into publishing by his son Adam Boyd Hamilton.

Hamilton Street in Harrisburg was named after three generations of Hamilton – John of Fermanagh, son Hugh and grandson Boyd. A John Hamilton of this family went to Texas, fought in the Mexican War there and gained a vast amount of property as a result of his service. Another John Hamilton in this family was active in the founding of Agricultural College of Pennsylvania, now known as the Pennsylvania State University. Hamilton County in Ohio was also named after the family.

When Boyd Hamilton wrote of the family in the 1870s he commented that the Hamiltons were uniformly more Scots-Irish Presbyterian than was common, even in that area of central Pennsylvania which was so thickly settled with people of this race. Other Scots-Irish names found in the ancestry of the Hamilton family are Alexander, Boyd, Buchanan, MacFarlane, Patterson and Young.

Chroniclers of the period spoke of the Scots-Irish settlers who arrived in central Pennsylvania in the decade after 1725 as folk "of the better sort . . . a Christian people". It was said that the rich and gracious Cumberland Valley became the centre of attraction for the Scots-Irish people for several decades.

Historian Wayland F. Dunaway described it thus: "This was the seed-plot and nursery of the Scots-Irish race, the original reservoir which, after having filled to overflowing, sent forth a constant stream of immigrants to the northward and and especially to the south and west. For a generation other racial groups were but scantily represented here."

The lands in the region were negotiated by the Scots-Irish in treaties with the Shawnee and Delaware Indian tribes, the deal known as the "Walking Purchase".

Acknowledging the *Ulster/American links:*

JIMMY CARTER (former U.S. President)
January 9, 1998

To Billy Kennedy,

Thank you for sending me a copy of *The Scots-Irish in the Carolinas.* I appreciate your thoughtfulness in remembering me, and send you my warm best wishes for happiness throughout the new year.

Sincerely,
Jimmy Carter.

EDWARD M. KENNEDY (Senator)
January 13, 1998

Dear Billy,

Vicki and I were delighted that you joined us in Carrickfergus. We greatly enjoyed visiting the Jackson Centre and learning from you more about the ties between the Protestants that left Northern Ireland and the United States. Many of those people and their descendants made great contributions to our country and we welcomed the opportunity to pay tribute to them. I enjoyed my history lesson – you do a great job.

With hopes for lasting peace in Northern Ireland.

Sincerely,
Edward M. Kennedy (Senator).

**EMBASSY OF THE UNITED STATES OF AMERICA,
LONDON**
January 21, 1998

Dear Mr. Kennedy:

Thank you so much for the books entitled *The Ulster Jacksons, The Scots-Irish in the Carolinas, The Scots-Irish in the Hills of Tennessee, The Scots-Irish in the Shenandoah Valley* and the *News Letter* which you presented to me during my recent visit to Carrickfergus with Senator Kennedy. Your kindness is much appreciated. The books both provide an insight into the Scots-Irish community in the United States and highlight the deep links between our two countries. My family and I look forward to learning more about those ties.

Please accept my best wishes.

Sincerely,
Philip Lader, Ambassador.

President Andrew Jackson, the son of a Co. Antrim Presbyterian couple who emigrated from Carrickfergus to America in 1765, said on a visit to Boston in 1833: *"I have always been proud of my ancestry and being descended from that noble race. Would to God, Sir, that Irishmen on the other side of the great water enjoyed the comforts, happiness and contentment and liberty that they enjoy here."*

20

Along the *Wilderness Road*

The Scots-Irish were prominent in the first flow of pioneer settlers who headed for Kentucky from the years immediately after the Revolutionary War. They came along the Wilderness Road, via the Ohio River and over the Cumberland Mountains to a region that many considered too dangerous to encounter.

By the late 1780s the population flow towards Kentucky moved at a rate of 10,000 a year - made up of English, Ulster-Scots, Scottish Highlanders, Welsh, German Lutherans and French Huguenots. The 1790 United States census revealed that close on 70,000 people had climbed on foot or on horseback over the steep path. The stream of immigrants increased to a flood, with some arriving by boat down the Ohio River from Pittsburgh. However, most took the safer overland route.

The early settlers of the mountains of Kentucky were principally an overflow from the great stream of immigration heading west from Pennsylvania, New York, New Jersey, Maryland, the Carolinas and Virginia. The main Kentucky settlements were at New River Valley and Big Sandy Valley, while some families spilled into central Tennessee at the Cumberland Plateau via the Clinch and Holstone Rivers.

Kentucky officially became the 15th state of the Union in 1792, but before that the Commonwealth of Virginia laid disputed sights on the territory.

A few days before the signing of the Declaration of Independence in 1776, Virginia, in adopting its constitution, seized the opportunity to claim jurisdiction over Virginia and the Northwest region, which included Kentucky. However, in 1782, a petition was submitted to Congress from the inhabitants of "a tract of land called Kentucky" which deemed themselves subjects of the United States and not of Virginia. By virtue of the Revolution the right of the British Crown to that territory had devolved on the United States and they asked Congress to establish them as a new state. It took a decade of intensive political wrangling to bring this about.

In 1763, a proclamation by King George 111 restricted English settlements to the eastern slopes of the Appalachian Mountains, but the desire of the pioneers to move westwards was overwhelming and by 1768 land negotiations were started with the northwestern Indians. However, while Kentucky had been surveyed for most of a century, it remained a land of mystery to the mid-18th century settlers in neighbouring Virginia and North Carolina.

The mystique was summed up a John Marshall, who wrote at the time: "The country beyond the Cumberland Gap still appeared to the dusky view of the generality of the people of Virginia, almost as obscure and doubtful as America itself to the people of Europe before the voyage of Christopher Columbus. A country there was . . . but whether land or water, mountain or plain, fertility or barrenness preponderated; whether inhabited by men or beasts, or both, or neither, they knew not. If inhabited by men, they were supposed to be Indians, for such had always infested the frontiers. And this has been a powerful reason for not exploring the region west of the Great Mountains, which concealed Kentucky from their sight."

For several centuries Kentucky was a battleground for territorial conflict between the Cherokee, Iroquois and Shawnee Indians and because of the stand-offs between the tribes the early white explorers experienced little resistance.

Gabriel Arthur, a long hunter from Fort Henry, is credited with being the first white man to see the land of Kentucky, known to the Iroquois Indians as Ken-ta-ke, meaning "Prairie" or "Meadow Land". He made the trip with a party of friendly Cherokees in 1674 and, after capture by the Shawnee Indians, he was allowed to return to Fort Henry provided he went back to the white men on the east coast to arrange a trade arrangement with the Shawnee. Arthur agreed, returning via the Cave Gap (the Cumberland Gap) to the Cherokee capital of Echota.

The Cumberland Gap was the popular crossing point in the Appalachian Mountain for the pioneering families heading into Kentucky. For centuries Indians had used the Gap as the Warrior's Path from the Potomac River down the south side of the Appalachians to the hunting grounds of Kentucky, Tennessee and Ohio. In 1750, Dr Thomas Walker discovered the Gap and mapped out its location, naming it and the Cumberland mountain range after the Duke of Cumberland, son of King George 11. Walker was a Virginian of Scottish descent.

Daniel Boone first sighted the Gap in 1769 after leaving his North Carolina farm with five hunting and scouting companions. After descending the western side of the Appalachian mountain range, Boone and his Long Hunter companions marvelled "from the top of the eminence, the beautiful level of Kentucke", a fertile land of cane and clover. They recounted stories about an abundance of game - "hundreds of acres principally covered by Buffelowes."

Boone had clearly fallen in love with Kentucky, with its level bluegrass fields and gentle cool streams. "I returned home to my family with a determination to bring them as soon as possible to live in Kentucke, which I had esteemed a second paradise, at the risk of my life and paradise," he later recalled.

After several trips through the Gap he returned in 1773 with about 30 woodsmen and with their axes they felled a road through the forest. The frontier was opened up to Kentucky, Tennessee and Ohio by virtue of Boone's Wilderness Road.

By 1800, it is estimated that three-quarters of the settlers moving into Kentucky, a big percentage of them Scots-Irish, made it there via the Cumberland Gap. It was a high-risk route for the settlers, for there was always the danger of attack from the Cherokee and Shawnee Indian tribes and from white renegades and marauders.

From the early 19th century the Cumberland Gap was used for transportation and commerce from east to west and today it acts as a link between Tennessee, Kentucky and Virginia.

During the Civil War of the 1860s the Union Army used the 1675-feet high and half-a-mile wide Gap - known as "the keystone of the Confederacy" - as the route into Tennessee. Both armies in the Civil

War believed that the invasion of the North or the South would come through the Gap and, from the two sides, they fortified the area against invasion.

Geologically the Cumberland gap is the result of dynamic earth stresses and movements from a bygone age. The north wide is of sandstone, shales and conglomerates, while the south side is of limestone which is said to contribute to the spectacular scenery and sheer cliffs.

The early years of pioneering life in Kentucky were marred by bitter conflict between the white settlers and the native Indian tribes, and the battles that were fiercely fought over land and territorial rights gave the state the unenviable title of "the bloody land".

It was a Cherokee Indian chief, Dragging Canoe, who first spoke of the region in such a gruesome manner when he warned North Carolina land speculators who came in 1768 to buy his tribal acres. He said: "We have given you a fine land, brother, but you will find it under a cloud — a dark and bloody ground."

The Kentucky lands were negotiated with the Indians by Colonel Richard Henderson, a North Carolina lawyer who was involved with the Watauga Association on the Holston River. Henderson formed the Transylvania Company and in 1775 he bought a 20,000,000-acre Kentucky tract from Cherokee chiefs for £10,000 worth of serviceable goods. The deal was struck between Richard Henderson and the Cherokee chiefs at Sycamore Shoals at Watauga, beside the present-day Elizabethtown in East Tennessee.

To cut a trail through the Cumberland Gap to provide access to the area, Daniel Boone was offered 2,000 acres and each of his 30 workers a smaller tract. The work was completed in a few months, opening the way for the pioneering settlers. Boone and his companions pushed northwards to the Kentucky River and they built a fort called Boonesborough. Kentucky had become an embryonic state.

Harrodsburg, on the banks of the upper Kentucky River, was the first permanent white settlement in the bluegrass state, coming about after a surveying mission led by James Harrod and Thomas Bullitt, who left Fort Pitt (Pittsburgh) in Pennsylvania in the spring of 1773 and descended the Ohio River to the mouth of the Kanawha River.

There, they met the Scots-Irish McAfee brothers - Robert, William, James and George, who had left Virginia on a similar mission. The two parties, numbering about 35 men, joined forces and proceeded via the

Ohio River to Salt River Valley, locating two settlements, one at Harrodsburg by James Harrod, and the other at McAfee's Fort a few miles north.They then returned to Pennsylvania and Virginia to plan for a migration in the following winter.

These early settlements had to withstand persistent Indian attacks, and there was also the problems of proving title to their lands, now that the Transylvania Company was claiming large portions through purchase from the Cherokees. During the Revolutionary War, Harrodsburg was the capital of Kentucky county, with a population in 1776 of 198 persons, of which 81 were eligible for military duty. Hugh McGary, the son of an Ulsterman, was the fort commander and a justice in Kentucky's first court.

Harrodsburg residents, most of them Scots-Irish, were said to be industrious and thrifty and in 1775 John Harman raised the first corn. The first woollen mill and first gristmill on the western frontier were operated here, and pottery, plows, flour and textiles were also manufactured. Like many of his frontier contemporaries, Daniel Boone was a farmer, blacksmith and a weaver, as well as being a long hunter.

To survive on the frontier everyone had to adapt and among the settlers there were carpenters, coopers, wheelwrights, wagonmakers, rope-makers, wine-makers, tailors, traders, surveyors and teachers.

The first school in the state was conducted within the fort in 1778. The teacher had no textbooks, and the children used smooth boards for paper and juice of ox galls for ink. However, they managed to read and write with remarkable proficiency, and patiently studied the Bible and the Presbyterian hymnals. By 1800, Harrodsburg was a prosperous community, with rich farm lands surrounding the town growing flax, hemp and tobacco.

John Adair, the eighth governor of Kentucky the son of Ulster-born parents, lived here as did other governors Gabriel Slaughter and Beriah Magoffin, and a governor of Georgia George S. Houston, as well as US senator John B. Thompson.

During the Revolutionary War, some Kentucky frontier settlements faced grave danger from British-backed Cherokee Indian attacks and in 1778 a 25-year-old Ulster-Scot General George Rogers Clark led a force of 175 men from Virginia to relieve the situation. The force covered 180 miles of swamp and forest to capture Kastaskia, Cahokia and Vincennes forts.

From these victories, the United States was able, in the Treaty of Paris, to obtain the lands northwest of the Ohio River. However, Clark and his men never received payment for their years of service to Virginia, despite frequent promises made.

Clark, born in Charlottsville, Virginia, was a surveyor for the Ohio company between Pittsburgh and Kentucky and he later served on a board that supervised allocation of 150,000 acres of lands in the Louisville area. After the War he conducted a campaign against the Wabash Indians.

A list of 4,000 names submitted on petitions addressed by early inhabitants of Kentucky to the General Assembly of Virginia throws interesting light on the composition of this population. Historians say they confirm a predominance of Scottish or Scots-Irish names, with a large number of English and some German, Dutch and French stock.

The Protestant non-conformist character of much of the population was evident and one pastor who was among the first to cross the threshold into Kentucky was Londonderry man the Rev John Brown, who had founded in 1755 the first classical school at Timber Ridge Presbyterian Church near Lexington in the Shenandoah Valley of Virginia.

Brown, who joined in the trek to Kentucky in 1775, wrote to his father-in-law Colonel William Preston, warning: "What a buzzel is amongst people about Kentuck! To hear people speak of it one would think it was a new found paradise; and I doubt not if it be such a place as represented but ministers will have thin congregations, but why need I fear that? Ministers are moveable goods as well as others and stand in need of good land as others do, for they are bad farmers."

Among those who moved in the early trek to Kentucky was Thomas Lincoln, who left Rockingham county in Virginia, married Nancy Hanks, and fathered Abraham Lincoln.

Early 20th century Kentucky historian William Henry Haney revealed that while English blood is predominant in the mountain people of the state, their amalgamation with the Scots-Irish "gave them greater courage, endurance and sturdiness to battle with the difficulties with which the pioneers of any country may contend."

In the minds of the frontier settlers, all men were free and equal, and should have due regard to the freedom and equality of others. They believed that the purpose of government was to ensure universal free-dom and equality. It was this philosophy which led to the formation of the Watauga association by Scots-Irish settlers in North Carolina/Tennessee in 1772.

The Watauga guidelines outlined the parameters for a decent, law-abiding Christian society, administered by the people.

The Kentucky mountaineers are in the main descended from soldiers of the American revolution, a great many of them Scots-Irish. The 35 mountain counties of Kentucky covering an area of 13,000 square miles had a total population of less than 10,000 before 1800 and in 1834 there were still living in the state nearly 500 War veterans from the 1776-83 period, most of whom had served in Virginia, North Carolina, Pennsylvania and Kentucky.

Overall, in the state of Kentucky there was, according to the 1790 census, a population of 75,000 and by 1800 the figure was 220,000. Remarkably, for 20 years after the settlement of Kentucky Daniel Boone's Wilderness Road through the Cumberland Gap was the only practicable route in and out of the state.

It was said that Kentucky was settled over the Wilderness Road, with 100,000 pioneers - a big percentage of them Scots-Irish - making the trek before it was properly converted into a wagon road.

* The Kentucky long rifle was the favoured weapon of Daniel Boone and the Scots-Irish frontiersmen. It was German gunsmiths in Pennsylvania who adapted imported Jaeger rifles for the specific fron-tier needs and they found a ready market for these west of the Appalachians.

The rifle barrel was lengthened to four feet for accuracy, the bore reduced in size to half an inch thereby saving on the amount of lead for the projectile ball, and the size of the sights increased. A grease patch was wrapped around the ball on a snug position in the barrel. It was said that a skilled marksman with a Kentucky rifle could put a bullet through a deer's head at 300 yards, while a man's head could be drilled at 250 yards. Kentucky rifles were used to good effect by the Scots-Irish operating from behind the bushes in the Revolutionary War.

A typical Scots-Irish family moving along the Wilderness Road.
Picture: H. David Wright, Nashville.

21

Pioneering Kentucky families *from Ulster*

THE LOGANS

Benjamin and John Logan, founding fathers of the state of Kentucky, were the sons of an Ulster-born couple David and Jane (McKinley) Logan, who settled at Augusta County (then Orange County) in the Shenandoah Valley of Virginia in the early 1740s after emigrating from the north of Ireland.

The Virginia and Kentucky Logans were said to be distant kinsfolk of Pennsylvania colonial treasurer James Logan, whose birthplace was Lurgan, Co Armagh, but while he was of Quaker stock the frontiersmen Logan clan were Presbyterians.

Benjamin and John were both baptised in 1743 and 1745 by the Rev John Craig, from Co Antrim, the first Presbyterian minister in the Shenandoah Valley. David Logan had been joined in the migrant trek by his brother James and as members of the Virginia militia they served in the French and Indian Wars. They were leading members of the New Providence Presbyterian Church in the Shenandoah Valley.

Benjamin Logan, as eldest son, inherited his father's entire estate in 1757, but instead of taking it for himself, he sold it and divided the proceeds among the other members of the family. As a land speculator, he kept buying and selling property and very soon had become one of the wealthiest people in the region.

On moving to the Holston River area of south-western Virginia he married Ann Montgomery and the family settled at Black's Station, the site of the present-day Abingdon in western Virginia near the Tennessee state border and close to North Carolina and Kentucky.

Logan was an adventurer in traditional Scots-Irish manner, enrolling in the Virginia militia when he was 16 and engaging in successful expeditions in north western Ohio against various Indian tribes. He also participated in the Governor Dunmore war campaign against the Indians in 1774, significant battles that opened up Kentucky for white settlements.

In the quest for the new lands, Logan was closely involved with Colonel John Donelson, of the Watauga movement of North Carolina and East Tennessee and the later father-in-law of President Andrew Jackson, and by James Knox , a surveyor and a hunter acknowledged as leader of "the leader of the Long Hunters".

In 1775, General Logan helped start a frontier stockade settlement called St Asaph in eastern Kentucky and, within a year, he became the first sheriff of Kentucky county and one of four militia companies. He led militia attacks on Shawnee Indian tribes along the Ohio River in 1781 and was elected to the Virginia assembly from Lincoln county, formed from part of Kentucky county.

Logan was a member of eight of the 10 conventions called to authorise statehood for Kentucky, including the final convention which wrote the state's constitution in 1792. The first state governor, Isaac Shelby, gave Logan a commission as a major general in the militia and he commanded a full division of soldiers. In 1792, Logan county, carved from part of Lincoln county, was named after him.

In every sense, Benjamin Logan was the archetypal frontiersman and at St Asaph's he worked from dawn to dusk, not only to economically sustain his family and the wider connections, but provide the necessary security in such a hostile environment. It is recorded that besides looking after his own interests, Logan marked tracts of land for his brothers and planted corn on each tract.

St Asaph's was extremely vulnerable to attack from the Cherokee Indians and vigilance had to be observed at all times by these hardy Scots-Irish settlers. Indian attacks were frequent, especially during the Revolutionary War period.

In one attack on May 23, 1777, Logan's Fort (St Asaph's) was besieged by a force of 100 Indians and some of the womenfolk, of necessity proficient with rifles, weighed in behind their husbands in resisting the assault. Other women assisted by moulding bullets, even using the small supply of pewterware at the fort when the supply of lead became scarce.

There were fatalities among the white settlers, including William Hudson, a close associate of Benjamin Logan, who had been out trying to round up the livestock. Logan personally rescued another of his guards Burr Harrison from the clutches of the marauding Cherokees. The injured Harrison, however, later died from his wounds, and with most of their livestock killed by the Indians, the settlers realised another attack was imminent.

Supplies were low, with gun powder a pressing need. It forced Benjamin Logan to head back to the Holston settlements in western Virginia for reinforcements, Another Indian attack was launched on St Asaph's in late August, but before the militia could get to the fort one of Logan's men Ambrose Grayson was killed and two companions wounded as they ventured out of the fort for corn supplies.

Interestingly, the Indians left on Grayson's body several copies of a British proclamation, signed by Colonel Henry Hamilton. In June, 1777, Hamilton had received instructions from London to deploy Indians against the white settlers, mainly of Scots-Irish origin, who were in revolt against the Crown. The proclamation offered food, lodging and humane treatment to all who deserted the American cause and presented themselves to any British post.

Those who would take up arms against the Americans and continue "until the extinction of the rebellion" were promised "pay adequate to their former stations in the rebel service". All common men who "shall serve during that period shall receive His Majesty's bounty of 200 acres of land".

Copies of the proclamation were discreetly shown to Benjamin Logan, who realised their implications for the morale of his men and he quietly hid them. An alliance had been forged between the British and the Indians and a cynical attempt was being made to buy off wavering white settlers. Clearly, Perfidious Albion was at work in all its machinations!

St Asaph's or Logan's fort was a dangerous outpost on the Kentucky frontier in the 1770s, but the raw courage of Benjamin Logan and his compatriots won through as a civilised and peaceful society in the state gradually emerged. Logan, who with his wife Ann had nine children — five sons and four daughters, died in 1802, after spending the last years of his life in constitutional politics as a Kentucky statesmen.

His brother John was also an army officer and he became the first state treasurer of Kentucky in June, 1792, a position he held until his death in 1807.

John's career as a soldier followed broadly the lines of Benjamin in the expeditions against the Indians and he held the rank of captain and lieutenant and colonel. He also represented Lincoln county in the Virginia legislature and was involved in the Kentucky statehood conventions. John Logan married Jane McClure, and they had six daughters and a son.

In 1795 John Logan, acting on authority from the first Governor of Kentucky, Isaac Shelby, joined a Scots-Irish associate James Knox in hiring surveyors and road cutters at two shillings and sixpence daily to improve access through the Cumberland Gap for the many migrant families pouring in from the east. They were aided in the task by Daniel Boone, then 61.

THE McAFEES

Robert Breckinridge McAfee, the leading Kentucky legislator and statesman of the early 19th century, was the grandson of Ulster pioneers James and Jane McAfee who emigrated to Pennsylvania about 1740.

The family eventually settled in Augusta county in the Shenandoah Valley of Virginia in 1748 and by 1779 they had put down their roots in Kentucky after years of exploration in the region alongside Daniel Boone.

The three sons of James and Jane McAfee - Robert, James Jun. and George - with Robert's brother-in-law James McCoun and a Samuel Adams risked threats from hostile Indian tribes on their frequent explorations into Kentucky. Even when the families settled at McAfee's station in Mercer county, Kentucky, they still suffered occasional casualties from Indian attacks. These were commonplace until the Indians were routed at the battle of Fallen Timbers in 1794.

Robert McAfee, who married his distant cousin Anne McCoun, was known as the "First Commodore of Western Rivers" for his operation of the first flatboats from the Salt River to the Ohio River and from there to New Orleans via the Ohio and Mississippi Rivers. Robert was murdered at New Orleans during one of these expeditions in 1795.

His son Robert Brackinridge McAfee became a guardian on the death of his parents to John Brackinridge, the attorney general of the United States in the cabinet of President Thomas Jefferson, and he graduated in law from Transylvania College in the 1790s.

McAfee was elected to the Kentucky state legislature and senate from Mercer county; became the state's lieutenant governor and emerged as an influential figure in Andrew Jackson's Democratic Party.

For five years, he served as charge d'affaires to the republic of Colombia in South America before returning to Kentucky for another term as state senator. His service as a captain in the militia during the War of 1812 was an obvious factor in his appointment to the board of visitors at West Point army base and he was elected board president. He was the author of the book, 'History of the War of 1812'. His wife Mary Cardwell was also from a Scots-Irish family.

The McAfee brothers founded the New Providence Presbyterian Church at Mercer county, naming it for what they saw as the work of providence during such a perilous time. New Providence was one of the first churches in this part of the American frontier.

THE BINGHAMS

This prominent Kentucky publishing family trace their roots back to Kilmore near Crossgar in Co Down to a Presbyterian farmer James Bingham whose sons emigrated to America about 1793, arriving in New York and moving on with their offspring through the States. The Binghams had crossed to Ulster from the north of England shortly after the Cromwellian wars of the 1650s, and the maternal side of the family was Scottish.

The Rev William Bingham, the eldest son of James Bingham, was the founder and first headmaster of the Bingham school at Wilmington, North Carolina.

This Glasgow-educated cleric ministered for a period in Co Down before emigrating in 1785 to start a career in teaching. He married Anne Jane Slingsby, the daughter of an officer in the British Army Colonel John Slingsby, and they had eight children. Bingham was also professor of ancient languages at the University of North Carolina for five years until 1805.

Thomas Bingham, a brother, arrived in America about the same time and he married Ulster-born Elizabeth McCann in Guilford County, North Carolina. They had 11 children, most of whom settled in Tennessee. Two other of the Bingham brothers Samuel and Joseph also emigrated.

From this family are descended subsequent headmasters of the Bingham School in Wilmington; Robert Worth Bingham, who was Mayor of Louisville, Kentucky and ambassador to Britain in 1933-37; George Barry Bingham, Senior and Junior, the editors and publishers of the Louisville Courier-Journal and the Louisville Times, and Sallie (Sarah) Bingham, the novelist.

Another of the Co Down Bingham kin was George Caleb Bingham, a celebrated painter of American western and frontier landscapes. He was born in Augusta county, Virginia and lived most of his life in Missouri. Bingham painted in 1850 "Daniel Boone coming through the Cumberland Gap with a band of pioneers", which acts as the appropriate cover for this book.

Robert Worth Bingham was the son of Colonel Robert Bingham, who ran a military college at Asheville, North Carolina. He was a lawyer who became an attorney in Jefferson county, Kentucky and was later Mayor of Louisville. In politics he was first a Republican before the First World War and then a Democrat in the 1920s.

In 1918 he purchased the Louisville Courier-Journal and Louisville Times, to which he added a printing company and a radio station, and through these outlets he actively campaigned for better public education and aid for blacks and poor rural whites in Kentucky.

President Franklin D. Roosevelt appointed him ambassador to the Court of St James in England in 1933 and, during his term, he enthusiastically promoted in Britain the post-depression policies of the Roosevelt administration.

His son George Barry Bingham Sen. inherited the media dynasty on his father's death in 1937, having work himself through the business as a news reporter, Washington correspondent and editorial writer. He served with the American navy during the Second World War and was public relations officer for US Naval Forces in Europe. He added television to the Bingham publishing chain and championed many causes, including civil rights, mental health, ethics and the environment. He was a close associate of Democratic politician Adlai Stevenson.

George Barry Bingham Jun. also headed up the family concern as editor and publisher, having earlier worked with the NBC network in Washington. He was in charge until the mid-1980s when the publishing interests were sold out of the family in a move that caused much trauma and commercial fall-out on the Kentucky scene.

Pennsylvania statesman, soldier and lawyer General Henry Harrison Bingham was also descended from Ulster Scots, but most probably he was no relation of the Kentucky Binghams. He was an officer of the 140th Regiment Pennsylvania Regiment during the Civil War and later a Republican member of the US Congress.

THE WARNOCKS

Co Tyrone man William James Warnock was a member of Daniel Boone's advance party which went up the Wilderness Road from the Yadkin River in North Carolina towards Kentucky in 1773.

Their purpose was to make settlement and establish homes for the party of six families and 40 men. However, William James Warnock did not reach Kentucky at this time largely due to an Indian ambush near the Cumberland Gap in which six of the party were killed, including Daniel Boone's son.

This disaster changed the plans for the party and they had to re-trace their steps to a settlement on the Clinch River, where they remained for some time. William James Warnock subsequently passed the barrier of the mountains and settled in Mason county, Kentucky. He and his wife Elizabeth Carlisle Warnock, had four sons, all of whom became extensive farmers. The Warnocks from Co Tyrone were a widely dispersed family, settling in Pennsylvania, Maryland, Virginia, North Carolina and Kentucky.

The Wilderness Road more or less followed the Old Warriors Path from North Carolina and Virginia through the Cumberland Gap to Kentucky. On late 18th century maps, this stretch is called "the old trail from the Old settle(ments) thro' the great wilderness".

THE McGARYS

Hugh McGary was another pioneer of Ulster stock who led his family through the Cumberland Gap with Daniel Boone. The McGarys had moved up with Boone from the Yadkin River in North Carolina into Virginia in 1775 and, although separated from the main party during Indian attacks, they made the Kentucky frontier post at Fort Harrod.

McGary was captain of the Fort Harrod militia and a justice in Kentucky's first court. His encounters with the Indians are part of Kentucky folklore and by the end of the Revolutionary War period he held the rank of colonel. Hugh operated from his own stockade at Shawnee Springs in Mercer county, Kentucky. His brother Martin married Andrew Jackson's cousin and with Jackson they became involved in many land schemes and skirmishing with the native American tribes.

Hugh McGary is believed to be a descendant of the McGary (or McGeary) family which moved to Pennsylvania from Ulster in the mid-18th century. They arrived in Philadelphia and immediately moved to the Cumberland Valley in central Pennsylvania, settling in West Pennsborough township.

Four McGeary brothers - Clemens, William, Neal and John - became extensive farmers in central Pennsylvania, with William, Neal and John fighting in the Revolutionary War. The family scattered in the trek westwards, with McGary (McGeary) family records traced to Ohio, Indiana, Arkansas, Tennessee, Texas and California.

THE WHITES

The White family was among the most enterprising, prominent pioneers of south western Virginia and south eastern Kentucky, distinctively Scots-Irish in culture and character.

The first-known emigrant from Ulster was John White and his wife Isabella, who settled at Harrisburg, Pennsylvania with sons Hugh and William, and a grandson Colonel James White became an important trader, businessman and manufacturer.

John White settled at Abingdon in Western Virginia and was a colonel (quartermaster) in the army of General Cox of Tennessee, whose duty it was to protect the white settlers on the frontier.

White manufactured iron furnaces in Virginia and Tennessee and carried on an extensive trade in the west. The interests extended into the salt production industry at Clay county, Kentucky and he soon became the wealthiest man in the region. On his death in 1838 his estate was valued at three-quarters of a million dollars, a fortune at the time.

A son Addison White was elected as a Whig to Congress in 1851 and was a Confederate officer in the Civil War. Princeton-educated and, of an academic streak, Addison engaged mainly in agricultural pursuits and cotton raising.

Colonel James Lowery White, brother of Colonel James, was also in salt manufacturing in Clay county, Kentucky and amassed considerable wealth and stature. He was a judge of the Clay county circuit and brigadier general of the Kentucky militia. His estate included 35 black slaves. Two of his sons — Alexander and John — served in the Kentucky house of representatives, with John, a Kentucky circuit judge, rising to become speaker of the United States Congress.

THE BLAIRS

This eastern Kentucky family can trace their ancestry back to Samuel Blair, who moved from Co Armagh in Ulster with his family in the early part of the 18th century, settling first in Pennsylvania, and then in Virginia. Two of Samuel's sons were pioneering clergymen - the Rev Samuel Blair and the Rev John Blair, while another of the family James was a distinguished lawyer.

The Rev Samuel Blair was educated at the Rev William Tennent's 'Log College' and his ministry remained largely in New Jersey. His brother John was also a graduate of the 'Log College' and he preached the doctrines of New Lights Presbyterianism, first in Pennsylvania and mainly in Augusta county in the Shenandoah Valley of Virginia, where he was instrumental in setting up 23 congregations. He was called to the chair of divinity in Princeton College and became vice-president of the university.

James Blair practised law at Abingdon in Virginia and he sat on the state legislature. However, he had itchy feet and migrated over Daniel Boone's Wilderness Road to Kentucky and established himself at Frankfort, the state capital, holding office as attorney general for Kentucky for 20 years (1796-1816). Blair was married to Elizabeth Smith, a grand-daughter of John Preston, a leading Virginia planter of Ulster stock.

A son Francis Preston Blair was a politician, journalist, lawyer and soldier who fought in the War of 1812 and when he re-entered civilian life became involved in the heady political issues of the period in Kentucky, including a move to expel the United States Bank from Kentucky through state taxation.

When he moved to Washington DC in 1830, Blair founded the Washington Globe newspaper, which was effectively the Democratic Party organ for President Andrew Jackson. He edited the paper until the Presidency of James Knox Polk.

Montgomery Blair, a son, was a lawyer, judge and statesmen, brought up in Lexington, Kentucky and trained as a soldier at West Point. He served as Mayor of St Louis, attorney general of Missouri; solicitor general of the US court of claims and was postmaster general in President Abraham Lincoln's cabinet in 1861-64.

Francis Preston Blair Jun. also practised law in St Louis, but moved west to become the first attorney general in New Mexico. When he returned to Missouri he served in the state legislature and had two terms in the US congress.

When the Civil War broke out Francis Preston Blair Jun. raised seven regiments for the Union Army and as a brigadier-general, and later a major general, he served under General William Sherman. He was an unsuccessful candidate for President at the Democratic convention in 1868. His statue stands at the Hall of Fame at Washington DC, by the side of another great Missourian, Senator Thomas Hart Benton, a life-long friend and kinsman.

Shenandoah Valley-born George Blair, another of the link to the Revs Samuel and John Blair was a pioneering farmer at Floyd county in eastern Kentucky, but because there was no Presbyterian church in his locality, he became involved with the Primitive Baptist Church.

Although he was a strict and honoured member of the church, it was said that very often he drank whiskey in excess. A son William was a Baptist pastor and mill owner.

American country singers, sisters Loretta Lynn and Crystal Gayle (nee Webb), are of the Blair connection in Eastern Kentucky and they express pride in their Scots-Irish roots.

THE MEEKS

This family emigrated from Ulster to Charleston in South Carolina in 1765 and in the Piedmont area Captain Adam Meek was a distinguished soldier in the Revolutionary War. Grandsons James and William Meek moved from North Carolina to the Big Sandy Valley in Kentucky, settling in Johnson county, and a son of James, the Rev Zephaniah Meek, was a prominent minister of the Methodist Episcopal Church of the South, and a prolific publisher. His son the Rev LaFayette Meek pastored in Tennessee.

THE POAGUES

Colonel Robert Poague and his wife and family of nine children (four sons and five daughters) left Ulster in 1738 and moved to Virginia by way of Pennsylvania, settling at Staunton in Orange county, subsequently Augusta county. Poague was commissioned as one of the first magistrates in this part of the Shenandoah Valley and was a captain in the Virginia militia from 1761. He was also the county surveyor.

A son, Major John Poague was high sheriff of Augusta county, while a grandson Colonel George Poague was the first of the family to migrate to eastern Kentucky, acquiring a vast tract of land along the Ohio River at Big Sandy Valley.

THE STEWARTS

This branch of the Stewarts came to Big Sandy Valley in Kentucky from Giles County, Virginia in 1813. Notables from the line of pioneer James Stewart kin were Colonel Ralph Stewart, a farmer and civic officer-holder, and the Honourable James E. Stewart, a lawyer, judge and public official who was jailed during the Civil War for expressing Confederate sympathies. He was the Kentucky attorney for six years and judge of the circuit court for a further six.

Engraved on the tombstone of pioneer Hugh Stewart in the cemetery of the Presbyterian Church at White Clay Creek Hundred, New Castle, Delaware is an interesting epitaph: "He loved each truth; his faith, love and faithfulness, none can to the life, as did his life express. Our new built church now suffers too, by the larger its windows but its lights are less."

Hugh Stewart (1685-1753) was an early Scots-Irish emigrant who was listed on the tax roll of New London township at Chester county, Pennsylvania in 1725. In 1734, he acquired for 176 pounds, 100 acres of land at watershed on both sides of White Clay Creek near New Castle, Delaware and witnesses to the deed were two Ulster immigrant brothers William and James McMechen.

The Stewarts became one of the most prominent families in this part of Delaware, with a son James and daughter Jannet, who married a John Stewart, moving to North Carolina, and a grand-daughter Jane, who married an Alexander Kirkpatrick, to Tennessee (Wilson and Sumner counties). Their sons were in the Revolutionary War.

THE ALLENS

Brothers John and Joseph Allen were born at Rockbridge county, Virginia into a Scots-Irish family who had moved into the Shenandoah Valley from Pennsylvania.

The family was among the first to reach Kentucky when the Cumberland Gap was opened up, arriving at Dougherty's frontier station at Boyle county in 1779 and eventually settling in Nelson county in 1784.

John Allen was a successful lawyer and married Jane Logan, daughter of General Benjamin Logan, the renowned Kentucky militiaman and politician. John was elected to the Kentucky General Assembly in 1800 and was commissioned a colonel in the Kentucky First Rifle Regiment to fight in Andrew Jackson's War of 1812. He was killed in action at the Battle of River Raisin in 1813.

Joseph Allen was also a lawyer and a county and circuit clerk. In the War of 1812 he served as a captain in the 8th Company of the Kentucky Mounted Volunteer Militia, declining the rank of colonel on the grounds that he lacked military experience.

The Allen Scots-Irish kin also distinguished themselves in Pennsylvania with General Harrison Allen from Warren county a Union army officer in the Civil War, fighting at various battles including Gettysburg. He later served as a Republican in the Pennsylvania state legislature; as state auditor-general and as US marshal for Dakota for four years. Robert P. Allen, from Lycoming county and whose mother Rachael Porter was of Ulster stock, was a prominent lawyer and state politician through the 19th century.

THE KENNEDYS

This prominent Kentucky family is descended from General Thomas Kennedy, who helped build Stove's Fort in 1779 and whose grandparents Captain Joseph and Elizabeth Kennedy emigrated from Ulster in 1733 to settle in Lancaster County, Pennsylvania and thence in Augusta county, Virginia. The two sons of the emigrant forebears John Kennedy Sen. and Dr Joseph Kennedy are recalled in historical annals as "the noteworthy set of pioneer Kennedy brothers."

John Kennedy Sen. was listed in 1770 as one of the earliest settlers of Rowan county, North Carolina, while his brother Joseph was the first trained doctor to practice in Mecklenburg county. He died in 1777 from wounds obtained in the Revolutionary War.

Joseph Kennedy, son of John Sen., also served in the War. General Thomas Kennedy captained the North Carolina Dragoons in the War and fought at the Battle of Kings Mountain. He was captured by the British and held for several years.

The Kennedys first came to Kentucky early in 1775, purchasing land from the Henderson company. General Thomas Kennedy was one of the first trustees of Boonesborough and, frequently, he had to use his considerable military experience to good effect to ward off Indian attacks. It is recorded that "the power of the Kennedy brothers" had much to do with the gaining of these valuable Kentucky lands from the native American tribes.

While absent on one occasion in 1781, Thomas Kennedy's fort at Paint Lick Creek was attacked and set on fire by marauding Indians. But his wife courageously put out the fires and, with others, she defended the fort successfully.

Early in the 19th century the Kennedy land of 10,000 acres stood out as one of largest estates in Kentucky. Thomas helped draw up the first constitution of the state in 1792 and he served in the Kentucky legislature for 25 years. He was one of the first to introduce the race horse industry in Kentucky and was acknowledged as one of sport's finest trainers.

THE JOHNSTONS (JOHNSONS)

This prominent Kentucky farming family trace back to Ulster-born Robert Johnston from Lancaster county, Pennsylvania, who married Lillias Corbett at First Philadelphia Presbyterian Church in 1737.

The couple and their family moved to Orange county, North Carolina in 1756 and, on Robert's death in the following year, a tract of 611 acres on the headwaters of the Rocky River was purchased in trust for Robert's three underage sons John, Robert Jun. and Thomas.

Thomas Johnston settled in Hawkins county, Tennessee in 1790 and further Johnston descendants eventually made it to Shelby Creek, Pike county in Kentucky around 1816, in the company of William (Preacher Bill) Tackitt and his family.

In a reference to a list of 4,000 or more names attached to petitions addressed by early inhabitants of Kentucky to the General Assembly of Virginia, American historian James R. Robertson makes this interesting statement: "The list of names is important for two main reasons; first, it throws light on the racial composition of the early population of Kentucky, and second, it is of use for the student of genealogy. The earlier petitions show a decided preponderance of Scotch and Scotch-Irish names with a large number of English and a few German, Dutch, and French. The number of English names increases in the later petitions. The large number of religious names indicates the nonconformist character of much of the population. While the list will not give much detail to aid the genealogist, it fixes the existence of a certain name in a locality at an early period and thus gives a clue that may be followed further."

22

Scots-Irish luminaries *of Kentucky*

JOHN ADAIR

John Adair, the eighth governor of Kentucky, was the son of Ulster-born parents William and Mary Moore Adair, who lived in Chester county, South Carolina and Charlotte, North Carolina after emigrating from Ireland.

For most of his life Adair was a political activist, who distinguished himself as a militiamen and in state and national office. Educated in the Scots-Irish stronghold of Charlotte, which Lord Cornwallis described as "the hornet's nest", this father of 12 children moved to Mercer county, Kentucky and it was from there that he occupied a pivotal role in the affairs of the state.

He was state representative and speaker of the Kentucky House and was a United States senator and congressman over different periods. He was elected governor in 1820 and, during his term of office, was instrumental in passing stringent gambling laws and abolishing imprisonment for debt.

His priority as a legislator was help for debtors who were in danger of losing their lands, something which appealed to his frugal Scots-Irish instincts and to this end he helped create the Bank of the Commonwealth. Having fought in the American revolution, John Adair was a major of volunteers in a campaign against the Miami Indians in 1791-92 and during the War of 1812 he was commander of the Kentucky rifle brigade at the Battle of New Orleans.

By 1817 he had become brigadier general of the Kentucky militia. Adair county in south- central Kentucky is named in his honour. John Adair of Kentucky is not to be confused with Co Antrim-born John Adair, who was one of the heroes at the battle of Kings Mountain in 1780 and later became one of the founding fathers of Knoxville in East Tennessee.

JAMES GILLESPIE BIRNEY

Kentucky statesmen and philanthropist James Gillespie Birney was the son of Ulster-born James Birney, who emigrated to Philadelphia in 1783 and prospered so well that in 1812 he was spoken off as the richest man in Kentucky. James Gillespie Birney was born at Danville, Kentucky in 1792, was a graduate of Princeton and returned to his home state to practise law. He was elected to the Kentucky assembly and won a reputation as an ardent anti-slavery politician.

Moving to Huntsville, Alabama, Birney was influential in shaping the constitution under which Alabama come into the Union and he served on the first legislature, opposing the endorsement of Andrew Jackson for the American Presidency.

Birney returned to Danville, Kentucky in 1830 to farm, but he became heavily involved in the movement for the emancipation of slavery and for the next few years he travelled the country for this cause, addressing large and enthusiastic audiences. He faced much opposition for his stance, particularly in Danville, and he was forced to move with his family to Cincinnati, Ohio, where he promised to keep up the agitation until slavery was abolished.

By 1837, Birney was secretary of the National Anti-Slavery Society, working out of New York and nearer the centre of power. He stood as anti-slavery candidate in the Presidential elections of 1840 and 1844. being heavily defeated with votes of 7,369 and 62,263.

ALEXANDER CAMPBELL

Ballymena, Co Antrim-born Alexander Campbell was a Protestant fundamentalist preacher who blazed a trail through the southern and eastern American states during the early 19th century.

Alexander was the eldest son of the Rev Thomas and Jane (Corneigle) Campbell and when the family emigrated to America in 1807 his father became pastor of a seceded Presbyterian congregation in Pennsylvania. The family followed in 1809 and that year the Campbells organised the Christian church of Washington as an independent denomination.

Ordained from Glasgow University, Alexander preached his first sermon in Pennsylvania in 1810 and with his father he set up a congregation of the Disciples of Christ at Brush Run, They were affiliated to the Redstone Baptist Association in 1815, but relations soured and the two factions broke away in 1820.

Alexander Campbell's extensive travels as an itinerant preacher took to him to Lexington in Kentucky and several of his congregations prospered there. He also had branches of the Disciples of Christ in Ohio, Indiana, western Pennsylvania and Virginia in the 1830s through to the 1860s, and by the time of the Civil War, the movement had an estimated 225,000 members.

Among the doctrines Campbell emphasised were the supreme authority of scripture, weekly celebration of the Lord's Supper, baptism of adults by immersion and independence of the local congregations, complemented by co-operation between congregations.

Campbell was a member of the Virginia constitutional convention of 1829, where he tried unsuccessfully to have slavery made illegal in the state. He did not consider slavery inherently wrong, because it was not condemned in scripture, but he viewed it as "expedient" and freed his own slaves. He did not believe in military solutions to political problems and remained neutral during the Civil War. Married in 1811 to Margaret Brown, he died at his home in Bethany, Virginia, now West Virginia.

JOHN CAMPBELL

John Campbell, was an American frontier entrepreneur and land speculator born around 1735 in Co Antrim. He came to Pennsylvania in 1755 with General Edward Braddock's British troops and engaged in the unsuccessful attempt to wrest Fort Duquesne (Pittsburgh) from the French during the French and Indian war of 1754-63. Fort Duquesne was later to fall to the British.

When the French were ousted from Pittsburgh in 1761, Campbell was listed as a "trader", and he emerged as one of the most successful fur traders on the frontier. He was also a backer of Virginia claims to the Pittsburgh territory and was a co-owner of large tracts of former Indian land in Ohio and Kentucky (Louisville).

During the Revolutionary War, Campbell was captured by the British and held in prison in Montreal for several years. On release, he resumed his trading activities in Kentucky and played a leading role in the framing of the state's first convention in 1792. He was a court justice and a senator for Jefferson county in Kentucky.

RICHARD BABINGTON FERGUSON

The Londonderry-born physician was an early pioneer in medicine in Louisville, Kentucky, emigrating to America as a young man in the late 18th century. Ferguson planned to travel to New Orleans, but, at the urging of a friend and the flip of a coin, he decided to stay in Louisville, then an emerging city of influence in the bluegrass state. Ferguson, who married Elizabeth Aylett Booth, and had seven children, helped organise Louisville's public health system and, in 1817, he became the only practising physician on the board of the city's hospital.

Kentucky Encyclopedia records confirm that in 1809 Ferguson assisted colleagues Dr William Galt and Dr John Collins in amputating the leg of Scots-Irish militia hero General George Rogers Clark, who survived the ordeal despite the lack of anaesthesia and antiseptics.

A fife and drum band was assembled to play martial music outside the room where the delicate surgery took place. Ferguson was a strong Christian and he helped found Christ Church Cathedral in Louisville. He died in 1853, aged 84.

ALBERT SIDNEY JOHNSTON

This renowned Confederate general of the American Civil War was of Ulster-Scots pioneering stock who had moved to Kentucky from New England in the early settlements of the state. Albert Sidney was born in Mason County, Kentucky, the son the village doctor, and in his early life he stood out as "a proud, manly, earnest and self-reliant boy". Johnston graduated from West Point Military Academy, where he formed a lasting friendship with Jefferson Davis, the Confederate President, which lasted until his death.

In 1832 he served throughout the Black Hawk War as a chief of staff, but two years later when his wife Henrietta Preston became seriously ill, and subsequently died, he left the army to take up farming.

He moved to Texas in 1836, then a fledgling republic under the presidency of another Ulster-Scot Sam Houston, and within a short time was elevated to the command of the First Texas Rifles, engaging in the various battles with the Mexicans. He was secretary for war in Texas in 1839, and expelled the intruding United States Indians after two battles on the River Neches.

Johnston withdrew from the army for several years to develop a farm plantation in Texas and continue his interest in the family Kentucky holdings, but he was again pressed into soldiering and was made a colonel of the US Second Cavalry by President Franklin Pierce. He led the Utah expedition by the military against the Mormons in 1858-60 and commanded the Pacific Department.

When the Civil War broke out in 1861, Johnston's sympathies lay with the Southern cause and at the time he was regarded by President Jefferson Davis as "the greatest soldier . . . then living". Johnston had early Civil War successes as he set about organising the Confederate Army, but after reverses at Forts Henry and Donelson there were calls for his removal as a general.

But he was defended by Jefferson Davis, who said: "If Sidney Johnston is not a general, I have none." His reputation was restored at the Battle of Shiloh in Tennessee in April, 1862 when he and his troops made a successful charge against Federal forces. It was during this charge that Johnston died from a leg wound, a loss which President Davis described as "irreparable".

JAMES CLARK McREYNOLDS

This great grandson of 18th century immigrants from Killyman in Co Tyrone was attorney general in the government of President Woodrow Wilson in the early part of this century, after having served as assistant attorney general in the White House regimes of Theodore Roosevelt and William Howard Taft.

Born in Elkton, Kentucky in 1862, James Clark McReynolds was descended from James and Mary Bell McReynolds who settled in Pennsylvania and the Shenandoah Valley of Virginia after the move from Ulster.

Mary's father Thomas Bell had been a shoemaker in Omagh, Co Tyrone, 20 miles from Dungannon, and was a Presbyterian elder there and when he moved to Pennsylvania.

The McReynolds family were Presbyterian stock and James and his son Thomas played a prominent role in the Revolutionary War in the Campbell county militia in Virginia, with wife Mary also cited as a patriot for her part in delivering supplies and ammunition to the front lines.

The bachelor James Clark McReynolds was the son of Dr John O. McReynolds, of Middle Tennessee, and he was a science student from Vanderbilt University in Nashville. He practised law in Nashville and taught at Vanderbilt University for several years. James Clark McReynolds became a highly influential figure in Woodrow Wilson's First World War administration, although he was considered difficult to deal with and had a belligerent streak. He was said to be proud, sensitive and aloof, the least popular in Wilson's government, but he was inscrutable.

A far distant cousin, who could also trace his family roots back to Co Tyrone, was Samuel Davis McReynolds, who during the administration of Franklin D. Roosevelt was leader of the House Foreign Affairs (Representatives) Committee.

Samuel Davis McReynolds was a Tennessean, born at Pikeville. He too was a lawyer who was a judge of the Criminal Court of Tennessee for 20 years before entering politics in 1923.

When he died in 1939, Sam McReynolds was paid this glowing tribute by President Roosevelt: "As a national legislator Sam McReynolds brought to his public duties exceptional ability, integrity, and great capacity for work."

23

Simplicity in the ways *of the frontier*

Everything about the early Scots-Irish settlers on the American frontier was characterised by a rugged outright simplicity - in their carb, the food they ate, the weapons needed for hunting and the tools used for working the land. In Joseph Doddridge's "Notes on the Settlement and Indian Wars of the Western Parts of Virginia and Pennsylvania" there is a graphic picture of their customs and manners portrayed by one of themselves.

"Most of the articles in common use were of domestic manufacture. There might have been a few things brought to the country for sale in a primitive way, but there was no store for general supply. Utensils of metal, except offensive weapons, were extremely rare and almost entirely unknown. The table furniture usually consisted of wooden vessels, either turned or coopered. Iron forks, tin cups etc. were articles of rare and delicate luxury. The food was of the most wholesome and primitive kind. The richest meats, the finest butter and best meal that every delighted a man's palate, were here eaten with a relish and labor only known. The hospitality of the people was profuse and proverbial.

"The dress of the settlers was of primitive simplicity. The hunting-shirt was worn universally . . . and was made of linsey, sometimes of coarse linen, and a few of dressed deerskin. The bosom of this dress was sewed as a wallet, to hold a piece of bread, cakes, jerk, tow for wiping the barrel of the rifle, and any other necessary for the hunter and warrior. The belt, which was always tied behind, answered several purposes besides that of holding the dress together. In cold weather the mittens, and sometimes the bullet-bag, occupied the front part of it. To the right side was suspended the tomahawk, and to left a knife in its leathern sheath.

"A pair of drawers, or breeches and leggins, were the dress of the thighs and legs, a pair of moccasins answered for the feet much better than shoes. These were made of dressed deerskin. They were generally made of a single piece, with a gathering seam along the top of the foot, and another from the bottom of the heel, with gathers, as high as the ankle joint. Flaps were on each side to reach some distance up the leg. Hats were made of the native fur; the buffalo fur was frequently employed in the manufacture of cloth, as was also the bark of the wild nettle."

The women dressed as simply as the men; their carb was a linsey gown, which they spun and dyed and fashioned themselves. For head-gear they wore huge sunbonnets, and on their feet moccasins like the men, or else went barefoot, as was largely the custom in the summer.

Historian the Rev. Henry C. McCook, in his "Scotch-Irish Women Pioneers", describes their character and work ethic: "Stalwart of frame no doubt they were, with muscles hardened under the strain of toil; hale and hearty, vigorous and strong, able to wield the axe against the trunk of a forest monarch or the head of an intruding savage; to aid their husbands and fathers to plow and plant, to reap and mow, to rake and bind and gather. They could wield the scutching knife or hackling comb upon flaxen stocks and fibres, as well as the rod of rebuke upon the back of a refractory child. They could work the treadle of a little spinning wheel, or swing the circumference of the great one. They could brew and bake, make and mend, sweep and scrub, rock the cradle and rule the household."

Living in the frontier environment, the Scots-Irish women were strong characters - self-reliant, resourceful, and loyal. Devout, patient, and cheerful in the midst of difficulties, they pursued the even tenor of their way, performing with efficient diligence the duties that lay nearest them.

24

Gospel fervour *in Kentucky and Ulster*

Religious revivals were a common event in the Appalachian states during the early 19th century and one of the most famous of these mass inspirational witnesses occurred in Kentucky in 1800, amongst a population predominantly Scots-Irish. The Kentucky spiritual movement has been likened to the 1859 Revival which took place in Ulster, mainly among the Presbyterian stock of counties Antrim and Down.

The centre of the 1800 revival was Logan County in south-west Kentucky, close to the Tennessee border and what was then known as the Cumberland country. This is a beautiful region, with a salubrious climate and fertile soil, a place where the Scots-Irish settlers who moved from Virginia and the Carolinas had no hesitation in making their home.

The Presbyterian segment of the population was the most numerous in Logan County and the revival that was initiated by pioneer preachers came within the bounds of the Transylvania Presbytery and the Synod of Kentucky.

The tendency to revivalism which got to the roots of fundamentalist Calvinism was strongly opposed by the leaders of the synod and some of those who initiated the movement were disciplined for alleged laxity and of practice.

The Rev. James McGready, the son of Ulster-born parents, was the man who ignited the spark of revivalism when he arrived in Logan

County from North Carolina in 1796. This doughty Scots-Irishman preached a modified Calvinism, dwelling on the necessity of the new birth and the importance of knowing the time when and the place where the conversion had occurred.

McGready was one of the founding fathers of the Cumberland Presbyterian Church, which had its origin in the Cumberland region of Tennessee and quickly spread into Kentucky and Virginia in the early 1800s.

The theology was similar in style to that practised by John Wesley and John Whitefield, the 18th century English preachers who spread the word through the eastern colonies of America. The message was clear and strong with impenitent sinners urged to seek immediate salvation in Jesus Christ. It was said of James McGready that he would "so array hell before the wicked that they would tremble and quake, imagining a lake of fire and brimstone yawning to overwhelm them and the hand of the Almighty thrusting them down the horrible abyss."

McGready became the minister of three small Presbyterian congregations - Gasper River, Muddy River and Red River. Logan County, like other frontier communities in the late 18th century, was a turbulent rumbustious society where so lax was the enforcement of justice that many law-breakers prevailed. Even among the law-abiding people in what was classified a Presbyterian settlement there was a significant degree of irreligion, with drunkenness a common trait. But when James McGready arrived the mood changed and a greater spirituality transcended the county.

From the preaching they heard folk speak increasingly of the need of the soul's salvation and news was noised abroad of the evangelical zeal of James McGready. In the summer of 1799 two McGee brothers, William, a Presbyterian, and John, a Methodist, arrived at Red River and from James McGready's gospel meetings they found the inspiration to develop a ministry which extended into neighbouring states. Other pastors who joined were, William Hodge, Samuel McAdoo and John Rankin.

The Rev. William Henry Foote, in his history of North Carolina and Virginia, recounts how the revival fires were lit by people who returned from McGready's meetings. From distances of up to 200 miles families came in covered wagons, equipped with food and bedding, to listen to the preaching at Red River, Gasper River and Muddy River settlements. The Gasper River gathering of the summer of 1800 was the first known religious camp-meeting in America.

James McGready had advertised the meeting as widely as he could and a huge crowd assembled, leaving the little church far too small for the throng. This despite the opposition of the Kentucky Presbytery, who viewed the movement as an attack on strict church doctrine.

The neighbouring forest was selected as the alternative venue and the pioneer worshippers, ready for any emergency, quickly cleared away the underbrush and felled the pine trees for pews. They improved a platform for the speakers over the day of toil and by dusk everything was in place for the gospel meeting which lasted from Friday to Tuesday.

The preaching, praying and singing continued without cessation except for a few hours in the morning, James McGready was assisted by other clerics in ministering to the many who came forward to declare themselves for Christ.

From the example of the Gasper River meeting, 10 other such camp-meetings were held in the region. Historical accounts relate: "Age snatched his crutch, youth forgot his pastime, and labourer quitted his task, the crops were left forgotten, the cabins were deserted, in large settlements there did not remain a soul".

Pioneer preachers brought religion and education to the frontier settlements. The preacher would often act as a doctor, he received no pay, and made his living off the land in the same way as the other settlers. He brought a simple message of the gospel.

The Ulster Revival of 1859 had remarkable parallels with the Kentucky experience of 1800, more than just the Presbyterian kin which bonded the communities on both sides of the Atlantic. It began in the Connor district of Co. Antrim close to the town of Ballymena as the result of a fellowship meeting in a butcher's shop. The revival spread to Ballymena and the neighbouring villages of Ahoghill and Broughshane and great congregations of several thousand people gathered in the open air, remaining all day in prayer and praise.

The revival spread to north of Coleraine and south into Co. Down and the favourite hymn "What's the News", with the word spreading swiftly from lip to lip. Many were converted to Christ.

The flame of Presbyterianism in Kentucky was lit by Welshman the Rev David Rice, who from 1783 gathered the scattered Presbyterians into regular congregations at Danville, Cane Run and the forks of Dick's River. He was followed by the Rev Adam Rankin, who gathered the church at Lexington; the Rev James Crawford, who settled at Walnut Hill, and by the Rev Andrew Craighead and the Rev Andrew McClure. These ministers formed the Presbytery of Transylvania with 12 congregations located over what was still a Kentucky wilderness.

Previous to the Rev Rice's arrival in Kentucky, marriages had been solemnised by magistrates, but this changed with the settlers making it obligatory to procure the services of a clergyman, for weddings and funerals.

Most of the early Presbyterian pastors in Kentucky had Ulster connections, with one the Rev Robert Marshall emigrating from Ireland to Pennsylvania at the age of 12. Marshall was a revolutionary war hero and after his ordination he took charge of the Bethel and Blue Spring congregations in Kentucky. He was an active leader in the great revival of 1800.

The Rev John Thomson, the son of an Irish-born Presbyterian elder, brought his family from Chambersburg, Pennsylvania to Kentucky in 1793 and was licensed by the Transylvania Presbytery. He became a pioneer missionary in Ohio, and later evangelised in Indiana. Of his seven sons, four became Presbyterian ministers - James, pastor at Crawfordsville, Indiana; John, professor at Wabash College, Indiana; William, a missionary of the American board at Beirut in the Middle East; and Samuel, another professor at Wabash College.

The Rev Robert Wilson who entered Kentucky as a missionary in 1798, was a second generation Ulsterman whose family has settled in Western Virginia. He organised congregations at Maysville, Augusta, Smyrna and Flemingsburg.

The Rev John Lyle, another of Scots-Irish stock from Rockbridge County in Virginia, was a missionary contemporary in Kentucky of Wilson and had charge of the Salem congregation. He established a female academy at Paris, Kentucky for 200 students about 1805.

25

Music transported *across the Atlantic*

B luegrass music that is centred on Kentucky and the neighbouring states of Tennessee, North Carolina, Virginia and West Virginia can be traced essentially back to the Scots-Irish who settled the region from the late 18th century.

These were a people who brought with them the old Scottish, Irish and English folk songs and ballads and, in remote communities in the Appalachian, Cumberland and Smoky Mountains, the songs stayed unaltered until the turn of the 20th century.

Music lightened the toil of the early pioneers, with the fiddle giving the lift at weddings and the jew's harp providing accompaniment along the wagon roads. The dulcimer was another favourite instrument on the frontier.

The fiddle, distinctively Scottish and Irish, was the main instrument for playing the tunes and providing backing for the traditional songs. Bluegrass music, as we know it today, became established with the wider American public in the 1940s when the late Bill Monroe first appeared with his acoustic band (a rich combination of fiddle, guitars, bass, dobro, mandolin and banjo!).

Monroe, from Rosine in Kentucky, became a household name throughout the States, emerging from Appalachian radio shows to become a national celebrity in American country music. He was of Scots-Irish ancestry and extremely proud of it; proud too of his home state and of perpetuating the idea of bluegrass being Kentucky music with songs such as Blue Moon of Kentucky, My Rose of Kentucky and Kentucky Waltz.

Others who followed the Bill Monroe line into bluegrass music with great success were Lester Flatt and Earl Scruggs, Bobby and Sonny Osborne, Ricky Skaggs (his family on his mother's side - the Fergusons - can trace their roots back to Londonderry and Donegal) and Jim and Jesse McReynolds, two Virginian musicians and singers whose Ulster ancestors came from Killyman in Co Tyrone.

Country rock duo The Everly Brothers (Don and Phil) hail from Brownie, Kentucky and they have gone on record in stating that their family roots were Scots-Irish. Dwight Yoakam is another country star with traditional Kentucky roots, born in Pikeville.

Bluegrass musicians place a high value on improvisation, generally playing their instruments by ear at a fast pace, in close harmony and with high pitched lonesome tenor vocals. The story theme centres on "the old mountain home" and of a people who are embedded into the rugged landscape of Kentucky and surrounding environs.

The Appalachian mountain people have maintained a folk-song culture for several centuries and leading balladeer and folk historian Cecil Sharp related in 1916 how that nearly every one he met in the mountain region, young and old, could either sing or play an instrument.

The ballads which Sharp collected in Kentucky, Tennessee, Virginia, the Carolinas and North Georgia were in the traditional vein, with Scots-Irish influences a very dominant strain. Popular Appalachian folk songs and tunes like The Girl from Knoxville, Barbara Allen, The Irish Washerwoman, Haste to the Wedding, The Virginia Reel and Turkey in the Straw came from that tradition.

The music of the American frontier was primarily vocal, through the singing of hymns and folk songs. In the very early settlements in Pennsylvania from the 1720s the fiddle provided the musical background for the reels and jigs which the Scots-Irish enjoyed. In the austere and at times lonely surroundings of the frontier, music was the source which brightened the lives of the settlers.

Fiddle styles varied from state to state, and even within states. Individual fiddlers differed in the way they held the instrument, the emphasis which they devoted to noting and the manner in which they bowed. Some fiddlers stuck resolutely to the melody, while others improvised freely or employed their own prepared techniques.

Richard Nevins, in his book Old-Time Fiddle Classics, notes that since fiddling was a Celtic art, modern aficionados strain to establish a direct link between Celtic styles and southern American renditions. "It is likely that all the countless variations in southern fiddling are traceable to seven or eight different styles brought over to America by predominantly Celtically cultured immigrants from various sections of the north of Ireland, southern Scotland and to to a lesser degree parts of England."

While yodelling has its origins in the Swiss mountains, many performers of a Scots-Irish background in states like Kentucky and Tennessee were adept at raising the tone to a falsetto head voice.

Gospel music was very dear to the hearts of the Scots-Irish and other God-fearing communities and many colloquial hymns, later adopted in mainstream Christendom, had their origins in the Appalachian region. And the Methodist evangelical hymns of Isaac Watts and John and Charles Wesley struck a chord with those moving along the Great Wagon Road to the new lands.

• The bluegrass region of Kentucky where many Scots-Irish families settled extends over the east-central and northern belt of the state, from Lexington to Louisville.

The region takes its name from the bluegrass plant (POA pratensis), which for centuries had been a major pasture grass on phosphatic limestone soils. This grass serves as grazing fodder for thoroughbred racehorses - another popular feature of Kentucky life - and it is also used as a covering for lawns and golf courses.

The Kentucky and Ohio Rivers traverse a large section of the region, which has a heavy corn and tobacco production.

Badge of Kentucky

The US *Constitution*
and the *Bill of Rights*

The US Constitution (ratified in 1788) placed the republic on a firmly federal basis. Its main provisions were:

1. A stronger central government divided into three branches - a President chosen by an Electoral College; a Federal judiciary; and a national legislature (composed of a popularly elected House of Representatives and a Senate chosen by the state legislatures).
2. While representation in the House was based on population, each state sent two delegates to the Senate.
3. Congress was given full power to levy import duties and taxes.
4. For representation and tax purposes a black slave was to be enumerated as three-fifths of a white person.
5. The African slave trade was not to be abolished before 1808.

The Bill of Rights (ratified in 1791) formed the first 10 amendments to the Constitution. These ruled against:

1. Abridgement of freedom of religion, speech, the press, petition, and peaceful assembly.
2. The infringment of the right to bear arms.
3. The illegal quartering of troops.
4. Unreasonable searches and seizures.
5. The capital trial of any person for the same offence; deprivation of life, liberty or property 'without due process of law'; self-incrimination; uncompensated seizure of property.
6. Infringement of an accused person's right to a speedy and public trial before an impartial jury.
7. Depriving persons of the right to trial by jury in common-law suits where the value in question exceeded $20.
8. Excessive bail and punishments.

Amendments 9 and 10 declared that the listing of certain rights in the Constitution should not be taken to deny others retained by the people, and reserved to the states all powers not delegated to the Federal government by the Constitution.

Thomas Jefferson described these rights as 'what the people are entitled to against every government on earth'. Several of them have been enshrined in the constitutions of other democratic countries.

26

Stephen Foster - *classical American composer*

C elebrated American songwriter Stephen Collins Foster was a
second generation Ulster-Scot whose family emigrated to
Pennsylvania from Londonderry in the late 18th century.
Stephen was born on July 4, 1826 near Lawrenceville, Pennsylvania,
now part of Pittsburgh and although he had little musical training he
had a great gift of melody and this was to strike the chord for lasting
fame worldwide.

As a six-year-old Stephen could play the clarinet and could pick up
any tune by ear. At 14 he composed The Tioga Waltz for piano and two
years later his first song Open Thy Lattice, Love was published.

Foster's first minstrel melodies were called "Ethiopian Songs" and
included Louisiana Belle and Old Uncle Ned. Minstrel shows, in
which white entertainers blackened their faces, were becoming popular in the United States and Stephen Foster provided the musical
scores.

While living in Cincinnati, Stephen wrote Oh! Susanna in 1846 and
this became the favourite song of the "Forty Niners" in the California
gold rush. The Foster songs were noted for their sincerity and simplicity and many became classics: My Old Kentucky Home, Massa's in de
Cold, Cold Ground, Campton Races, Beautiful Dreamer and Jeannie
With The Light Brown Hair, a number inspired by the composer's wife
Jane McDowell.

Stephen Foster compiled more than 200 songs and wrote the words
and the music for most of them. After his marriage to Jane McDowell,

Foster returned to Pittsburgh and worked full-time as a composer. Some of his tunes were adapted, with suitable words for Sunday school use.

He had an arrangement with minstrel leader E.P. Christy to have his songs performed on the stage, but his lack of business acumen led to many of his most famous songs being sold for very little money. In the latter years of his life, Stephen Foster tragically struggled against illness, poverty and alcoholism and he died in 1864, tragically a man of little means.

The Foster musical legacy, however, has stood the test of time and today it has an honoured placed in the American folk tradition.

Another famous composer in the United States with Ulster connections was Jimmy Kennedy, who was born in Omagh, Co. Tyrone in 1902. Jimmy wrote a huge selection of songs that were to become classic standards for singers such as Gene Autry and Bing Crosby. They included South of the Border, Red Sails in the Sunset, The Teddy Bear's Picnic, Isle of Capri, Roll Along Covered Wagon, Harbour Lights, Did Your Mother Come From Ireland?, The Cokey Cokey, Down the Trail of Achin' Hearts and Blaze Away.

Francis Scott Key, the man who wrote the American national anthem, was also of Scots-Irish stock. Key, a leading Washington lawyer and amateur verse writer, found inspiration for the words of 'The Star-Spangled Banner' during the War of 1812.

When the British retreated from Washington during the war, they took Key's friend William Beanes with them. In response, Key received permission from President James Madison to intercede with the British for the release of Beanes. He boarded a prisoner-exchange boat in September, 1814 that was held in temporary custody by a British warship. From this vantage point behind enemy lines, Key witnessed the British fleet's bombardment of Fort McHenry in Baltimore Harbour. He watched the shelling with anxiety throughout the night. The next morning, he saw that "our flag was still there" despite the ordeal. His joy inspired him to write a poem about it.

Key forwarded the text to a Baltimore printer after being released by the British. He borrowed the tune from a popular English drinking song 'To Anacreon in Heaven'. The American Congress adopted the song as the national anthem in 1931.

Key, born in Frederick County, Maryland, practised law in Frederick. He became district attorney of the District of Colombia in 1833 and in that year, President Andrew Jackson sent him to settle a land dispute with the Creek Indians in Alabama. Key remained district attorney until 1841. He never took his poetry seriously, though he wrote enough to fill a collection, Poems of the Late Francis S. Key, Esq (1857). Much of his poetry was religious, and included the hymn, "Lord With Glowing Heart I'd Praise Thee". He was once interested in becoming an Episcopal clergyman.

The Scots-Irish Presbyterians made a striking contribution to the campaign for religious freedom in America during the 18th century.

Prior to the Declaration of Independence, all persons, even dissenters, were required to pay contributions to the established church. But the Declaration of Independence made this seem incongruous so that many ministers were in a quandary what to do. At the first meeting of the Hanover Presbytery in Virginia after the adoption of the Declaration of Independence, a memorial to the legislature of Virginia was prepared setting out cogent reasons for complete separation of church and state.

This memorial closed with the following appeal: "Therefore we ask no ecclesiastical establishments for ourselves: neither can we approve of them when granted to others. This indeed would be giving exclusive or separate emoluments or privileges to one set of men, without any special public services, to the common reproach and injury of every other denomination."

After a bitter debate in which Thomas Jefferson support-ed the Presbyterian memoralists the law for separation was passed December 5, 1776. Separation was advocated not by those who desired to destroy religion but by the Presbyterians, the Baptists and the Quakers. There was no intention to weak-en religion but to make it a matter of free choice.

The Winning *of the West*

President Theodore Roosevelt was a prolific writer on American frontier life in the 18th century and a great admirer of the Scots-Irish character and pioneering spirit. In his classic work "The Winning of the West", Roosevelt explains the rudiments of the forts and stations where the frontier families sheltered during Indian attacks.

"When a group of families moved out into the wilderness they built themselves a station or stockade fort; a square palisade of upright logs, loopholed, with strong blockhouses as bastions at the corners. One side at least was generally formed by the backs of the cabins themselves, all standing in a row; and there was a great door or gate, that could be strongly barred in case of need. Often no iron whatever was employed in any of the buildings. The square inside contained the provision sheds and frequently a strong central blockhouse as well. These forts, of course, could not stand against cannon, and they were always in danger when attacked with fire; but save for this risk of burning they were very effectual defences against men without artillery, and were rarely taken, whether by whites or Indians, except by surprise. Few other buildings have played so important a part in our history as the rough stockade fort of the backwoods.

The families only lived in the fort when there was war with the Indians, and even then not in the winter. At other times they all separated out into their own farms, universally called clearings, as they were always made by first cutting off the timber. The stumps were left to dot the fields of grain and Indian corn. The corn in especial [sic] was the stand-by and invariable resource of the western settler; it was the crop on which he relied to feed his family, and when hunting or on a war trail the parched grains were carried in his leather wallet to serve often as his only food. But he planted orchards and raised melons, potatoes and many other fruits and vegetables as well; and he had usually a horse or two, cows, and perhaps hogs and sheep, if the wolves and bears did not interfere. If he was poor his cabin was made of unhewn logs, and besides the large living and eating-room with its huge stone fireplaces, there was also a small bedroom and a kitchen, while a ladder led to the loft above, in which the boys slept. The floor was made of puncheons, great slabs of wood hewed carefully out, and the roof of clapboards. Pegs of wood were thrust into the sides of the house, to serve instead of a wardrobe; and buck antlers, thrust into joists, held the ever-ready rifles. The table was a great clapboard set on four wooden legs; there were three-legged stools, and in the better sort of houses old-fashioned rocking-chairs. The couch or bed was warmly covered with blankets, bear-skins, and deer-hides."

27

Scots-Irish ties *to the Cherokees*

The relationship on the American frontier between the Scots-Irish and Indian tribes like the Cherokees was volatile at times, but in many pioneering settlements there was a marked degree of peaceful co-existence and mutual harmony with the natives.

President Andrew Jackson, who initiated the movement of the Cherokees and other tribes from their lands in the 'Trail of Tears' expedition to Oklahoma in 1834, is not best remembered in the native American folklore. But others of Jackson's ethnic origin have found an honoured place with a people whose proud culture and way of life was virtually decimated over two centuries of United States expansion.

James Adair (1709-83), who was born in Co. Antrim, is remembered primarily as a recorder of Indian history in his book 'History of the American Indians', published in London in 1775. Adair, of Scottish lowland origin, was considered a diplomat and a peacemaker among the Indian tribes of the south east which included the Cherokees, Siouans, Catawbas, Creeks, Shawnees, Choctaws and Chickasaws.

Adair emigrated from Ulster in 1735, landing at Charlestown, and from his tavern at Cherokee Ford in South Carolina he traded with the Indians. In his book, James theorised that the Indians were descended from the lost tribes of Israel and his detailed observations at close hand made the publication valuable to ethnologists and students of 18th century literature. His account of Indian manners, customs and language is widely recognised even today. Like many white settlers of his generation he left numerous offspring among the Cherokee.

Adair in his book 'History of the American Indians' confirmed that he resided with the Overhill (or Western) Cherokees in the Tennessee Country, whose settlements were on the Tennessee River, and its branches. This covered the 1737-43 period and in 1744 Adair transferred his residence to the Chickasaw nation in what is now North Mississippi. The Chickasaws extended to the Savannah River region in North Georgia/South Carolina.

It was among his "cheerful brave Chikkasah" that Adair rose to prominence as a trader and a diplomat. Their innate independence and bravery appealed to him and it was said that theirs was a kinship of spirit. The Chickasaws had a strong dislike of the French and James Adair joined the tribes in bloody forays against enemy Indians, particularly the Shawnees, who were then siding with the French.

Historians describe James Adair as a man of liberal education, which extended to mastery of the Hebrew language. It was said he was a good diplomat in dealing with his inferiors, but was not diplomatic in his attitude towards those who were officially his superiors.

An acridity of speech, an unsmooth temper and not a little vanity brought him into conflict with superiors when he deemed himself untreated. He remained ardent in his friendship of the Chickasaws, and recognised in that tribe: "love of the land, constancy in hatred and friendship, sagacity, alertness and consummate intrepidity".

James Adair had a manuscript of his book published several years before the date of the actual London publication of 1755. On September 7, 1769 the South Carolina Gazette recorded: "An account of the origin of the primitive inhabitants and a history of those numerous warlike tribes of Indians, situated to the westward of Charlestown and subjects hitherto unattempted by any pen.

"Such an attempt has been made by Mr James Adair, a gentleman who has been conversant among the Cherokees, Chickasaws, Choctaws, etc, for thirty-odd years past; and who, by the assistance of a liberal education, has written essays on their origin, language, religion, customary methods of making war and peace etc". It was also announced that Adair was " going over to England" soon to prepare for publication".

The following month both the South Carolina Gazette and the Savannah Georgia Gazette published Adair's prospectus of the book, proposed to be sold by subscription. These included essays on the origin, history, language, religion, customs, civil policy, methods of declaring and carrying out war, and of making peace, military laws, agriculture, buildings, exercise, sports, marriage and funeral ceremonies, habits, diets, temper, manners etc of the Indians of the continent of North America, particularly of the several nations or tribes of the Catawbas, Cherokees, Creeks, Chickasaws and Choctaws, inhibiting the western parts of the colonies of Virginia, North and South Carolina and Georgia.

Adair's work has been cited widely as a basic authority by the leading ethnologists and historians of America. In Winsor's 'Narrative and Critical History of America' it is described as a work of great value, showing the relations of British traders to the Indians, and is of much importance to the student of Indian customs.

Logan in his 'History of South Carolina', said that from Adair's book the world had derived most that is known of the manners and customs of the southern Indians. "Its style is exceedingly figurative and characteristic and partakes much of the idiom of the Indian dialects to which the author was so accustomed."

As for Adair and his theory of the Jewish origin of the American Indians, many writers and commentators of the period, before and after, held this view and the argument is chronicled in many books and pamphlets.

Soon after the discovery of America, the theory was advanced that the Indians derived from the lost tribes of Israel. Garcia, in his Origen de las Medianos (1607), declared that these tribes passed Behring Strait and made their way southward. He claimed to have found many Hebrew features in the native American languages.

Presbyterian ministers brought the Christian mission to Cherokees on the frontier, the most notable cleric being Scotsman the Rev. William Richardson, who for many years lived among the tribes.

The Scots, particularly the highlanders, maintained a pragmatic relationship with the Cherokees in the Carolinas and Tennessee and ties became so close that Indians began to bear names like Ross, McIntosh and McDonald. John Ross, the chief of the Cherokees for 50 years up to the period of the 'Trail of Tears', is the offspring of Scottish trader Daniel Ross, and John McIntosh, also a Cherokee luminary, is the grandson of another trader, Lachlan McIntosh.

The 'Trail of Tears' involved the displacement of thousands of Indians from the south east to Indian territory in Oklahoma and points west. In May, 1830, President Andrew Jackson signed into law the Indian Removal Act, thus putting teeth into the policy his predecessors had long advocated – the "voluntary" exchange of lands by eastern Indians for territory that the federal government would acquire for them west of the Mississippi. Jackson gave the policy immediacy and an assertion that existing Indian treaties did not constitute federal recognition of Indian sovereign rights to the soil of their homelands.

The Removal Act did not authorise the use of force – but neither did Andrew Jackson feel obliged to protect Indians from any force mobilised by the states and their citizens. The government had long before promised Georgia that it would to eliminate Indian title to the lands within its boundaries in exchange for the state's western land claims.

The demands of Georgia, and of the white speculators, planters, and farmers eager to take over Indian land, mattered far more to Andrew Jackson than any guarantees made to Indians in treaties.

So, when Georgia unilaterally extended its laws over the Cherokee nation in 1829, Jackson withdrew federal troops and denied protection to the Cherokees. In 1830 Cherokees who held tribal office automatically became criminals. Georgia prepared to distribute their lands by lottery, and seize their other property for debt. They had little recourse against fraud or theft since, as Indians, they could not testify in Georgia's courts.

The Cherokee government withdrew to the town of Red Clay in Tennessee and John Ross, the principal chief of the Cherokees, led a complicated legal fight against state usurpation of their sovereignty and the federal government's refusal to enforce treaty provisions.

They won a legal victory of a sort and in 1832 the U.S. Supreme Court upheld treaties as "the supreme law of the land," and ruled that Georgia's laws did not apply within the Cherokee nation. Federal marshals could not act to enforce the ruling until a state judge formally refused to comply, and in this case the state simply ignored the Supreme Court, which adjourned without ever reporting to the

President Georgia's failure to conform. As a result, the decision had no practical effect.

This left the Cherokees and the other southern tribes at the mercy of the states. Alabama and Mississippi followed Georgia in extending their laws over the Indian nations, and North Carolina and Tennessee did likewise For the Choctaws, Chickasaws, Cherokees, and Creeks the result was a disaster. From self-governing peoples living on their own lands, Indians became a people impoverished by the government with no right to protect their lives or property.

The federal government held out removal as the only realistic hope for renewed security and sovereignty, and in desperation and anguish southern Indians were left to "choose". The large majority of Indians in the south had no desire to move, but after 1832 they had no effective way to resist. In each Indian nation there were those who saw removal as inevitable. Some viewed it as a way of escaping whites; some saw personal or factional gain in co-operation; some simply resigned themselves to obtaining the best price they could.

Ulster-Scots luminary, Sam Houston, the once Governor of Tennessee and Texas, was so attracted to the Cherokee Indian ways that he cut himself off from his family in Blount County, East Tennessee and went to live with the tribes for two years.

The Cherokee chief Oolooteka, known as "John Jolly" befriended Sam, who was given the title "The Raven". Sam, a teacher, adopted their dress and customs and mastered the Cherokee language, considered to be one of the most difficult in the world. The Indian sojourn earned Sam reproachment from his brothers for deserting the family, but, although he tired of the Indian ways, it was not to be the last time that he aligned himself with the Cherokees.

In 1829, on the break-up of his first marriage in Murfreesboro, Middle Tennessee, Sam returned to the Cherokee settlements and was welcomed back by Chief John Jolly (Oolooteka) and given a certificate of adoption by the tribe.

Once again, Sam took on the dress, customs and manners of the Cherokees and he hunted, fished, attended war councils and, in keeping with the tribesmen, drank to excess, earning him the ignominious title of "Big Drunk".

During this three-year period with the Indians, Sam Houston visited Washington several times on their behalf and, dressed in Indian garb, he was warmly welcomed by President Andrew Jackson. He also cohabited with a half-breed Indian woman Tyania Rodgers Gentry and it was said he left her only when she refused to desert her people. After this, Sam moved in 1833 to the Rio Grande and Texas.

Sam Houston was the grandson of an Ulster Presbyterian from East Co. Antrim, the region where President Andrew Jackson's parents left for America in 1767.

In many ways Scots were the best group able to empathise with Native Americans. Scots saw similarities between themselves and Indian society. Both Scots and Indians followed a clan system. Both had a tremendous sense of identity with nature and the environment. Neither viewed land ownership as individual. Both the gaelic language and native American tongues were spoken and not written until relatively recently. Both languages were rich in imagery and there developed a close association between Scots and Indians.

Scots and Irish generally treated the tribes fairly in business affairs. Many intermarried with the Cherokee, and the progeny is now part of the modern Cherokee population. But intermarriage had some negative results as well. Mixed-blood leaders were more prone to acculturation, adopting the white man's ways.

Acculturation also had a negative impact on the status of Cherokee women. In traditional Cherokee society, women, due partly to the Cherokee matrilineal kinship system, had an equal vote with men in council meetings, as well as being all-powerful over war captives.

With acculturation and the adoption of a constitution very similar to that of the United States, women were relegated to an inferior status, with no right to vote and with little control over land and family. Cherokee women became "as subservient, oppressed, and powerless as their white sisters."

Many Scots and Ulster settlers left records both official and unofficial, which are invaluable in reconstructing Cherokee history and culture of the 18th century with Adair the most prolific.

One of the items most demanded by the Cherokee from Scot, Irish, and other European traders, was the gun. Guns swapped with the Indians were know as "trade guns". They were lighter and preferred by the Indians, who wanted a weapon easy to carry.

However, they broke down quicker and had a larger bore, requiring special shot. The use of these trade guns made certain the dependency of the Indians on the white man. Guns were extremely important for the Cherokee; they facilitated the hunt and, together with the acquisition of horses, extended rather rapidly the Cherokee hunting range.

Equally important, the Cherokee needed guns because their Creek enemies had guns. Without guns they would be at a decided military disadvantage. The Cherokee could kill deer as a means of buying guns to defend themselves, or else the tribe could face being killed or enslaved.

In the early 18th century, the Cherokee traders on more than one occasion encouraged the Cherokee to wage war for slaves and to fight on the English side against the French and Spanish. The Cherokees were important as a barrier against the French and Spanish, and they tried to use this rivalry to their own advantage. They allied themselves with the English in return for trade goods.

The French and Indian War ended the French threat. Unfortunately, it also ended the importance of the Cherokee as a barrier. By the end of the Revolution War when the British were driven out of America, the Cherokee and other Indians lost their last realistic opportunity to play one side against the other. The Cherokee then had to play the losing game of dealing with the more powerful new America nation, which was steadily increasing its demands for more land.

The Scots and Irish, as well as the English, increased the frequency and the reasons for war. In fact, the Cherokee War of 1760-61 might have been avoided had the South Carolina governor attempted to understand Cherokee culture. He failed to realise that the demand placed on the Cherokee to surrender 22 men responsible for the murder of 22 white settlers was impossible.

Such a demand could not be met without the approval of those individual clan members, and that approval was highly unlikely. The governor also failed to see who had killed 22 Cherokee in Virginia was evened out by the wrong of the Cherokee killing an equal number of settlers.

Fighting beside and against whites changed traditional Cherokee tactics. The Cherokee normally fought for revenge or in retaliation, usually killing the same number of enemy that the tribe had lost earlier. By 1817, the Cherokee attacked an Osage village in Arkansas while the men were away. The Cherokee actually "killed women and children, stole livestock and property, and took about 100 captives and burned the village," activities unheard of in earlier days.

Traditional Cherokee tactics had been replaced by methods that "came to resemble those of the United States Army." The frequency of war also brought a decline in population, and as long as the Indians were fighting one another, the threat of Indians unifying against whites was lessened.

As early as 1725, the Cherokee reported that they had become dependent on white trade. This dependency restricted Cherokee independence, since unfavourable actions might result in trade sanctions.

Trade goods and "a better kind of hatchet," as one legal historian has put it, helped bring about a decline in the traditional crafts of the Cherokee. Trade goods brought by Scots, Irish, and other traders also helped destroy Cherokee values of subsistence and equality. Prior to white contact, equality had existed among the Cherokee; "getting ahead" was a white concept.

Of course, there were some Cherokees who were better off than others, but the difference was never great – that is, until the appearance of the white man. Cherokee often obtained goods from traders on credit and these debts led to land cessions in the late 18th and early 19th century.

Besides increased warfare, the white people's disease, especially smallpox, had a devastating effect on the Indians. Whites had been exposed to these diseases for centuries and had built up an immune system against them. Cherokee and other native Americans did not have this immune system, and whole villages were wiped out when exposed to these diseases.

Probably their first exposure to these European diseases came in 1698, when a smallpox epidemic decreased their population measurable. In 1738, another smallpox epidemic destroyed approximately one half of the total Cherokee population.

Normally, the Cherokee went to their medicine men for cures, but they had no power against these new diseases. As a result, the power of these figures declined. Often medicine men believed the failure lay in their ritual paraphernalia. Believing this had lost its power, the medicine men threw it into the fire. Since medicine men were unable to provide a cure, the Cherokees tried a traditional method of purification – a sweathouse followed by plunging into an icy stream.

This practice only added to the number who died. Others who survived the disease were horror stricken by their disfigurement and killed themselves, rather than live in disgrace. White people's diseases, brought by the Scots-Irish and others, were especially harsh on the elderly. With the expected death of their elders, much of Cherokee history and oral tradition was lost.

In addition to population losses, the 1739 epidemic had other consequences. Towns were relocated and Cherokee distrust of the English, whom they thought were responsible for the disease, increased, allowing the French to get a foothold among the Cherokees.

In 1760, an invading army led by the Scot Archibald Montgomery brought another epidemic of smallpox. In 1780, an epidemic hit the Cherokees again, while still another smallpox epidemic in 1783 broke their last remaining resistance to the advancing white settlement of their lands.

The impact of the Scots and Irish on the Cherokee was far-reaching. The Scots and Irish did help record and preserve Cherokee culture, but they also helped destroy traditional beliefs and social status. They affected population sizes, changed settlement patterns, and altered traditional roles for Cherokee men and women.

The Cherokees survive today in spite of the white man, with communities still intact in parts of North Carolina and Tennessee. They are rebuilding and rediscovering their heritage and traditions. The positive and negative effects of Scottish and Irish contact have both helped and hindered the Cherokee search for their traditional heritage.

"Murder is murder and somebody must answer, somebody must explain the streams of blood that flowed in the Indian country in the summer of 1838. Somebody must explain the four thousand silent graves that mark the trail of the Cherokees to their exile. I wish I could forget it all, but the picture of six-hundred and forty-five wagons lumbering over the frozen ground with their cargo of suffering humanity still lingers in my memory. Let the historian of a future day tell the sad story with its sighs, its tears and dying groans. Let the great Judge of all the earth weigh our actions and reward us according to our work."

JOHN G. BURNETT
United States Army and interpreter on the
Trail of Tears of 1834

Indian tribes on the Trail of Tears to Oklahoma in 1834.
Picture: Robert Lindneux.

28

The Crocketts from Ulster,
plus letters from home

The name Crockett on the American frontier conjures up immediately the image of the legendary Davy, whose fame 200 years ago extended far from his native East Tennessee as a hunter, soldier and politician. Davy's grandfather David came from the North Tyrone/East Donegal part of Ulster and he passed through the Shenandoah Valley before settling in the Holston River region of North Carolina and East Tennessee.

Davy was born in a one-room log cabin in a valley at Limestone in Greene County, East Tennessee on August 17,1786. His grandparents were massacred by Indians as they were putting crops in the fields at Carter's Valley (the site of the present-day town of Rogersville) in November, 1777. Davy was a scout for General Andrew Jackson in the Creek War of 1813-15 and became a colonel in the Tennessee militia. In politics, he served in the Tennessee legislature and was elected twice to the US Congress. He died in 1836 bravely defending Fort Alamo from Mexican aggression.

Other Crocketts moved from Ulster about the same time, and we know of a Robert Crockett, from Co Antrim, who sailed to America with his wife Margaret in 1730. Historical records show that their child, John Crockett, was "born upon sea near Pennsylvania shore." John's headstone at the Old Waxhaw Presbyterian Church at Lancaster, South Carolina relates: "Lived in America til almost fourscore; happy the man who has his sins forgiven, by our Redeemer who now lives in Heavn."

Robert Crockett moved from Pennsylvania to Orange or Augusta County and was one of the first to purchase land in the Beverly Manor tract at Staunton in the heart of the Shenandoah Valley. His settlement ran to 322 acres and when he died in 1747, aged only 40, this was dispersed among his six sons and one daughter. Some of the family stayed in Virginia, but others moved on to Kentucky, Tennessee and South Carolina.

LETTERS FROM HOME IN ULSTER

John Forsythe, who emigrated from Artikelly near Limavady in Co Londonderry in 1773 and settled at Birmingham township in Chester County, Pennsylvania, maintained contact with his family back in Ulster through regular correspondence.

In one letter from his father John dated June 25, 1788, Forsythe is acquainted of the death of his mother and his grandmother. The letter reads: "With greef I must Let you know that your Dr Mother have Departed this life the 19th June by aling-gren Disorder of six months. She had her sences to the last and died in Hope. Your brothers and sisters are all well. Your Grandmother Cox died some monts ago."

Letter writing was quite a penchant in the Forsythe family and John's brother Jacob and sisters Catherine, Jane and Sally kept up the news from home. In one letter, a friend in Artikelly Richard McCammon wrote in 1801 to inform that the price of "victuls of every kind" had been very high for two years: "oat meal at 7 shillings 7 pence per score; barly male 6 shillings; potatics 4 shillings 4 pence per bushel". Words were spelt as they were pronounced.

Correspondence was coveyed across the Atlantic on the ships which ferried the immigrants to their American destination and returned to the Ulster ports when their human cargoes were delivered. It could have taken as long as three months for a letter to be delivered, but for the folks on both sides of the Atlantic it was well worth waiting for.

29

"No Eerish *bot Scoatch*"

Scots-Irish settlers in America were always at great pains to distinguish themselves from the native Irish who emigrated and in religion and culture, as in their former homeland, they broadly ploughed a different furrow.

Parker's history of Londonderry, New Hampshire from the 18th century relates: "Although they came to this land from Ireland, where their ancestors had a century before planted themselves, the Scotch-Irish settlers retained unmixed the national Scotch character. Nothing sooner offended them than to be called Irish. Their antipathy to this appellation had its origin in the hostility there existed in Ireland between the Celtic race, the native Irish and the English and Scotch colonists."

The Rev. James MacGregor, minister of Aghadowey in Co. Londonderry and a defender of Londonderry during the 1688-89 Siege, wrote to Colonel Samuel Shute, Governor of New England colony, along the same lines shortly after arrival from Ulster in 1718 with several hundred Presbyterians from the Bann Valley around Coleraine, Ballymoney and Macosquin.

"We are surprised to hear ourselves termed Irish people, when we so frequently ventured our all for the British Crown and liberties . . . and gave all tests of our loyalty which the government of Ireland required, and are always ready to do the same when required."

The Rev. Dr John MacIntosh, of Philadelphia, and an Ulsterman, made this statement: "From Derry to Down I have lived with them. Every town, village, and hamlet from the Causeway to Carlingford is familiar to me.....It has been said that the Ulster settlers mingled with the Celt....The Ulster settlers mingled freely with the English Puritans and with the refugee Huguenots; but so far as my search of state papers, old manuscripts, examination of old parish registers, and years of personal talk with and study of Ulster folk disclosed - The Scots did not mingle to any appreciable extent with the natives....To this very hour, in the remoter and more unchanged parts of Antrim and Down, the country folks will tell you: 'We're no Eerish bot Scoatch.' All their folk-lore, all their tales, their traditions, their songs, their poetry, their heroes and heroines, and their home-speech, is of the oldest Lowland types and times."

The early wave of Ulster-Scots Presbyterian families to America had still strong attachments to the British Crown, but these sentiments largely dissipated over the years of the 18th century until the Revolutionary War period when most of this ethnic ground was considered hostile to British interests.

Nevertheless, for all the sensitivities it still touches upon, the term "Scotch-Irish" has an historical reality and utility. Ulsterman Francis Mackemie (Makemie), the founding father of the Presbyterian Church in America, was enrolled in the University of Glasgow in February, 1676 as "Franciscus Makemus Scoto-Hyburnus".

The form "Scotch-Irish" would have been used in the vernacular, as "Scotch" was the proper idiom until the 20th century for both language and people. "Scotch-Irish" had been used for the Ulster-Scots in America as early as 1695, but usually in a figurative way.

The early Presbyterians from Ireland generally knew themselves simply as "Irish" and were thus known by the other colonists. The later establishment and rapid growth of highly visible and voluble Irish Roman Catholic communities led many Protestants in the United States to adopt the Scotch-Irish label.

Today, of the estimated 40 million people in the United States with Irish blood in their veins, an estimated 56 per cent trace their roots back to the 18th century Ulster-Scots settlers.

30

Anti-slavery movement *of Appalachia*

The anti-slavery movement in America began among the Scots-Irish Covenanters, largely in North Carolina, East Tennessee and Kentucky, 20 to 30 years before there was any organised opposition to slavery elsewhere, even in the supposedly enlightened and liberal New England of the period.

In 1800 the Rev. Dr. Alexander McLeod hesitated at accepting a call to the Covenanter congregation in Chambers Street, New York, because 20 of the members held black slaves. Thereupon, the Covenanting Presbytery enacted that "henceforth no slaveholder should be retained in their communion".

By 1815, the Presbyterian Covenanters, the Methodists and the Quakers of East Tennessee had 18 emancipation societies. A few years later there were six in Kentucky, and by 1826 there were 143 emancipation societies in the United States, of which 103 were in the south. Not one was in Massachusetts. John Rankin, the noted Covenanting anti-slavery leader, said in 1820 that it was safer to make abolition speeches in Kentucky or Tennessee than in the north.

East Tennessean Elihu Embree is generally acknowledged with writing the first pamphlet in the United States for freeing the slaves. Elihu, son of a Pennsylvanian Quaker Thomas Embree who held a similar outlook, was born in Washington County in Tennessee after his family moved to the area. Embree was educated by second generation Ulsterman the Rev. Samuel Doak, who conveyed the divine message to the Scots-Irish-dominated militia before the Battle of Kings Mountain in October, 1780.

Embree, although a slave-holder himself, was vigorously outspoken in his opposition of the practice and in 1817 he delivered two memorials to the Tennessee legislature on slavery. Later in 1819, through his weekly newspaper 'The Emancipator', operating out of Jonesboro in East Tennessee, Embree devoted his columns totally to freeing the slaves.

The paper had a circulation of 2,000 subscribers, many of whom were the Scots-Irish settler families of the region and it was significant that slavery was not widely practiced in this part of Appalachia. Slavery was much more prevalent in Middle and West Tennessee where the large plantations were situated.

Slavery was a dominant issue from the birth of the American nation and, while many politicians expressed revulsion at the practice, they realised the economic dependence on it. President George Washington freed his slaves in his will and Thomas Jefferson proposed total abolition in 1800.

The United States Congress outlawed slavery in all its territories in 1862 and a preliminary Emancipation Proclamation was formalised on January 1, 1863 to free "all slaves in areas still in rebellion."

It was a President of Co. Antrim stock, Andrew Johnson, who ratified the ending of slavery on December 18, 1865. The 13th Amendment to the American Constitution stated: "Neither slavery or involuntary servitude, except as a punishment for crime whereof the party shall have been duly convicted, shall exist within the United States or any place subject to their jurisdiction."

An *American view*

"Arnold Toynbe theorised in his epic "A Study of History" that a civilisation would eventually fall if it was not stimulated by outside competition. We can relate this theory to the religious institution of the Presbyterian Ulster-Scots, that is the Scotch-Irish. When they were living in Scotland and Ireland, the animosity to their Protestant Reformed faith from the established Church of England and the Roman Catholic Church was constant and severe, but it never overwhelmed them. It only strengthened their resolve to be Presbyterian. Yet when they reached America there was no such antithesis. So eventually they mellowed. Also, the Presbyterians insisted on highly-educated ministers. When the Baptists and the Methodists came along with their less-educated, fiery evangelists they made deep inroads into those who called themselves Presbyterians. So the Scotch-Irish of today are in the majority Baptist, secondly Methodist and thirdly Presbyterian. To pay their passage, over to the New World, nine out of ten sold themselves as indentured servants. This worked out well as an introduction into a new land. They initially poured into Pennsylvania and then southwards through the up-country of Virginia, the Carolinas and into Georgia. The largest settlements were in Virginia and the Carolinas. Yea, even to this day, it's a rare longtime resident of this area of South Carolina, North Carolina and Georgia, and other Appalachian states, who doesn't have some Scotch-Irish genes and chromosomes."

Dr WILLIAM H. HUNTER
family practice physician, journalist and author
- Clemson, South Carolina.

American frontier campfire. Picture H. David Wright, Nashville

Author's *acknowledgments*

- John Rice Irwin, Museum of Appalachia, Norris, Tennessee
- Gerald Roberts, Shannon Wilson, Sidney Farr and Harry Rice - Special Collections Department, Berea College, Kentucky
- Loyal Jones, Berea, Kentucky
- Mark Wetherington, Director, The Filson Club Historical Society, Louisville, Kentucky
- Dr Richard K. and Eva McMaster, Elizabethtown, Pennsylvania
- Mary Karnes, Donegal Presbyterian Church, Elizabethtown, Pennsylvania
- Tom and Romaine Campbell, Elizabethtown, Pennsylvania
- Alister McReynolds, Principal, Lisburn College, Co Antrim
- James and Karen Duncan, The Scotch-Irish Society of the United States of America, Vineland, New Jersey
- Tomm Knutson, Greenville, South Carolina
- Lynn R. McR. Hawkins, Bluff City, Tennessee
- Ellen Thomasson, Missouri Historical Society, St Louis, Missouri
- Stevan Jackson, Director Appalachian/Scottish/Irish Studies, East Tennessee State University, Johnson City
- Charles F. Moore, Center for Appalachian Studies, East Tennessee State University, Johnson City
- Cherel Henderson, East Tennesse Historical Society, Knoxville
- Tommy Rye, Maryville, Blunt County, Tennessee
- John and Carole Lebert, Knoxville, Tennessee
- Hugh Hamilton, Merion Station, Pennsylvania
- Susan E. Carter, Kennett Square, Pennsylvania
- Florence McClure, Las Vegas, Navada
- Robert David McClure, Belfast

- Barbara Parker, Department of Tourist Development, Tennessee
- Philip Lader, US Ambassador, London
- Robert O. King, Greenville, South Carolina
- Dr Katharine Brown, Museum of American Frontier Culture, Staunton, Virginia
- Professor Michael Montgomery, University of South Carolina, Columbia
- Ralph R. Parke, Edgewood, Kentucky
- Robert Anderson, (Printer), Richhill, Co Armagh
- Geoff Martin, Editor, Ulster/ Belfast News Letter
- Councillor Dr Ian Adamson, Belfast
- Muriel Millar Clark Spoden, Kingsport, Tennessee
- Dr Charles Moffatt, Gallatin, Tennessee
- Chris McIvor, Librarian, Ulster-American Folk Park, Omagh, Co Tyrone
- Christine Johnston, Ulster-American Folk Park, Omagh, Co Tyrone
- Linda Patterson, Ambassador Productions/Causeway Press, Belfast
- Dr William Hunter, Clemson, South Carolina
- Rev. Ernest E. Logan, Groomsport, Co. Down
- Rev. Dr. Leslie Holmes, Pittsburgh, Pennsylvania
- Robin Greer, US Consulate Office, Belfast
- Rosemary McGeary, New York
- H. David and Jane Wright, Nashville, Tennessee
- David M. Johnson, San Francisco, California
- Anne Martin, Limavady, Co. Londonderry
- Fred Brown, Knoxville News Sentinel, Tennessee
- Cherith Caldwell, Belfast
- Councillor George Shiels, Maghera, Co. Londonderry
- Arthur G. Chapman, Portadown, Co. Armagh

Bibliography *and references consulted*

- The Scotch-Irish in Western Pennsylvania by Robert Garland
- Pittsburgh: The Story of an American City by Stefan Lorant
- Mellon House - National Trust Committee for Northern Ireland 1970
- The Mellons by David E. Kosnoff
- Thomas Mellon and his Times - Centre for Emigration Studies, University of Pittsburgh
- Autobiographical Album of Prominent Pennsylvanians
- Colonial and Revolutionary Families of Pennsylvania by Wilfred Jordan
- The Fair Play Settlers of West Branch Valley (1769-84) by George D. Wolf
- Pioneer Outline History of North Western Pennsylavania by W. J. McKnight
- The Growth of Democracy (1740-1776) by Theodore Taylor
- The Planting of Civilisation in Western Pennsylvania by Solon J. Buck and Elizabeth Hawthorn Buck
- From Ulster to Carolina by Tyler Blethen and Curtis Wood Jun.
- Carolina Cradle: Settlement of the Northwest Carolina Frontier by Robert W. Ramsey
- Encyclopedia of Dauphin County, Pennsylvania
- History of Dauphin County, Pennsylvania
- Pennsylvania, The Colonial Years (1681-1776) by Joseph J. Kelley Jun.
- History of Pennsylvania by William H. Egle
- Biographical Album of Prominent Pennsylvanians
- Daniel Boone and the Wilderness Road by Bruce H. Addington
- Daniel Boone, Master of the Wilderness by John Bakeless
- The Wilderness Road to Kentucky by George H. Doran
- Kentucky: A Guide to the Bluegrass State
- Kentucky Biographical Dictionary

- The Kentucky Encyclopedia by John E. Kleber
- History of Kentucky, Volume 1
- Kentucky Settlements and Statehood (1750-1800) by George Morgan
- Historic Families of Kentucky by Thomas Marshall Green
- Early Families of Eastern and South-Eastern Kentucky
- Pioneer Families of Eastern and South Eastern Kentucky by William C. Kozee
- Selected Readings: Appalachian-Scottish-Irish Studies, East Tennessee State University
- Land of the Free: Ulster and the American Revolution by Ronnie Hanna
- The Scotch-Irish: A Social History by James G. Leyburn
- The Encyclopedia of the South by Robert O'Brien
- Encyclopedia of the American Revolution by Mark M. Boatner 111
- John Adair's History of the American Indians
- American's First Western Frontier: East Tennessee by Brenda C. Calloway
- John Peebles' American War 1776-1782 by Ira D. Gruber
- The Overmountain Men by Pat Alderman
- Colonists from Scotland by Ian Charles Cargill Graham
- Pioneers of Destiny by W. D. Weatherford
- Religion in the Appalachian Mountains by W. D. Weatherford
- Scotch-Irish Pioneers in Ulster and America by Charles Knowles Bolton
- Princetonians (1769-1775) by Richard A. Harrison
- Kentucky descendants of James Bingham, of Co Down, Northern Ireland by James Barry Bingham
- History of The Religious Society of Friends in Lurgan by Arthur G. Chapman
- The Scotch-Irish of Colonial Pennsylvania
- Primitive Traits in Religious Revivals by Frederick Morgan Davenport
- The Scot in America and the Ulster Scot by Whitelaw Reid
- The Pioneers of Mifflin County, Pennsylvania
- Pennsylvania History, Volume 38
- History of the the Sesquehanna Region and Paxtang Church
- The Southern Highlander and his Homeland by John C. Campbell
- Conestoga Wagon: Masterpiece of the Blacksmith by Arthur L. Reist
- Gods's Frontiersmen: The Scots-Irish Epic by Rory Fitzpatrick
- Complete Book of United States Presidents by William A. Degregorio
- Who Was Who in the Civil War by John S. Bowman
- Ulster Emigration to Colonial America (1718-1775) by R. J. Dickson
- The Great Wagon Road by Parke Rouse Jun.
- Stories of the Great West by President Theodore Roosevelt
- Donegal Presbyterians by Richard K. McMaster

- The Wataugans by Max Dixon
- Belfast News Letter, 250 Years (1737-1987)
- Westering Man, The Life of Joseph Walker by Bil Gilbert
- First Pittsburgh Presbyterian Church: The Church That Was Twice Born by Rev Ernest E. Logan
- First Pittsburgh Presbyterian Church: The Church That Kept On Being Born Again by Rev Ernest E. Logan
- History of the Lost State of Franklin by Samuel Cole Williams
- James Buchanan and his Family at Wheatland, Lancaster, Pennsylvania by Sally Smith Cahalan
- James Buchanan: Bachelor Father and Family Man by Philip Shriver Klein
- The Century Illustrated Monthly Magazine (1884-1885), New York
- Records of Lancaster County Historical Society, Pennsylvania
- Scotch-Irishwomen Pioneers by H. C. McCook
- How Scotch-Irish is Your English? by Professor Michael Montgomery

NOTE OF AUTHORITY:

"The Session of First Presbyterian Church, Pittsburgh grants Mr Billy Kennedy permission for one time use of photographs and written materials from our official history books for his book on the influence of the Scots-Irish in Pennsylvania"

Rev Dr Leslie Holmes (Minister),
Andrew D. Bogard (Clerk of Session).

PICTURES AND ILLUSTRATIONS

- Missouri Historical Society, St Louis
- Donegal Presbyterian Church, Elizabethtown, Pennsylvania
- First Presbyterian Church, Pittsburgh, Pennsylvania
- James Buchanan Foundation, Wheatfield, Lancaster, Pennsylvania
- Ulster/Belfast News Letter
- H. David Wright, Nashville, Tennessee
- Filson Historical Society, Louisville, Kentucky
- Tom Campbell, Elizabethtown, Pennsylvania
- Northern Ireland Tourist Board

Presidents *of the United States*

Order /Name	Party	Home State	Term	Profession
1. George Washington	Federalist	Virginia	1789-97	Planter/soldier
2. John Adams	Federalist	Massachusetts	1797-1801	Lawyer
3. Thomas Jefferson	Republican	Virginia	1801-09	Lawyer
4. James Madison	Republican	Virginia	1809-17	Lawyer
5. James Monroe	Republican	Virginia	1817-25	Lawyer
6. John Quincy Adams	Republican	Massachusetts	1825-29	Lawyer
7. Andrew Jackson	Democrat	North Carolina	1829-37	Lawyer/soldier
8. Martin van Buren	Democrat	New York	1837-41	Lawyer
9. William Harrison	Whig	Virginia	1841	Soldier
10. John Tyler	Whig	Virginia	1841-45	Lawyer
11. James Knox Polk	Democrat	North Carolina	1845-49	Lawyer
12. Zachary Taylor	Whig	Virginia	1849-50	Soldier
13. Millard Fillmore	Whig	New York	1850-53	Lawyer
14. Franklin Pierce	Democrat	New Hampshire	1853-57	Lawyer
15. James Buchanan	Democrat	Pennsylvania	1857-61	Lawyer
16. Abraham Lincoln	Republican	Kentucky	1861-65	Lawyer
17. Andrew Johnson	Democrat	North Carolina	1865-69	Tailor
18. Ulysses Grant	Republican	Ohio	1869-77	Soldier
19. Rutherford Hayes	Republican	Ohio	1877-81	Lawyer
20. James Garfield	Republican	Ohio	1881	Teacher
21. Chester Alan Arthur	Republican	Vermont	1881-85	Lawyer
22. Grover Cleveland	Democrat	New Jersey	1885-89	Lawyer
23. Benjamin Harrison	Republican	Ohio	1889-93	Lawyer
24. Grover Cleveland	Democrat	New Jersey	1893-97	Lawyer
25. William McKinley	Republican	Ohio	1897-1901	Lawyer
26. Theodore Roosevelt	Republican	New York	1901-09	Lawyer
27. William Howard Taft	Republican	Ohio	1909-13	Lawyer
28. Woodrow Wilson	Democrat	Virginia	1913-21	Teacher
29. Warren G. Harding	Republican	Ohio	1921-23	Journalist
30. Calvin Coolridge	Republican	Vermont	1923-29	Lawyer
31. Herbert Hoover	Republican	Iowa	1929-33	Lawyer
32. Franklin D. Roosevelt	Democrat	New York	1933-45	Engineer
33. Harry S. Truman	Democrat	Missouri	1945-53	Lawyer
34. Dwight D. Eisenhower	Republican	Texas	1953-61	Soldier
35. John F. Kennedy	Democrat	Massachussetts	1961-63	Author
36. Lyndon B. Johnson	Democrat	Texas	1963-69	Politician
37. Richard Millhouse Nixon	Republican	California	1969-74	Lawyer
38. Gerald Ford	Republican	Nebraska	1974-77	Lawyer
39. James Earl Carter	Democrat	Georgia	1977-81	Farmer
40. Ronald Reagan	Republican	Illinois	1981-89	Actor
41. George Bush	Republican	Massachussetts	1989-93	Politician
42. William Clinton	Democrat	Arkansas	1993-	Lawyer

• Grover Cleveland served two terms

Index

A

B

THE SCOTS-IRISH CHRONICLES
By Billy Kennedy

The Scots-Irish in the Hills of Tennessee
(First Published 1995 and now in four prints)

Centred in Tennessee, this is the absorbing story about a race of people who created a civilisation in a wilderness and helped lay the sole foundations for what today is the greatest nation on earth. The Scots-Irish Presbyterians who settled in the American frontier during the 18th century were a unique breed of people with an independent spirit which boldly challenged the arbitrary powers of monarchs and established church prelates.

The battles with the British forces, the native American tribes and the elements in a climate that had its extremes, took a terrible toll on the men, women and children, but with a doggedness and steely character inherent in their culture, the brave Scots-Irish pioneers won through.

The book records for posterity the daring exploits of a people who tamed the frontier. It is a story that needs to be told, retold and told over and over again so that the light of democracy and freedom can shine brightly in the complex world in which we live.

The Scots-Irish in the Shenandoah Valley
(First Published 1996)

The beautiful Shenandoah Valley alongside the majestic backdrop of the Blue Ridge Mountains of Virginia is the idyllic setting for the intriguing story of a resolute people who tamed the wilderness of the American frontier. The Ulster Presbyterian stock, or the Scots-Irish, as they were known, created a civilisation in the Shenandoah during the 18th century that was to be the springboard for further frontier advance and settlement to the west.

In the Shenandoah Valley, the Scots-Irish were real achievers and leaders in their community, church and state. American President Woodrow Wilson came of this ilk; so too did distinguished American Civil War generals Thomas Jonathan "Stonewall" Jackson and J.E.B. Stuart; innovative farm reaper inventor Cyrus McCormick; celebrated author Mark Twain (Samuel Langhorn Clemens), and soldier/statesman General Sam Houston, the Governor of Texas and Tennessee.

The Ulster-Scots were a breed of people who could move mountains. They did this literally with their bare hands 200 years ago, winning the day for freedom and liberty of conscience in the United States.

The Scots-Irish in the Carolinas
(First Published 1997)

The Carolina regions of the United States of America were settled in large numbers during the 18th century by tens of thousands of Ulster-Scots Presbyterians, who left their native shores for reasons of religious persecution and economic deprivation. In this the third of his absorbing series on the hardy Scots-Irish communities who tamed the wilderness of the American frontier, journalist-author BILLY KENNEDY heads on a journey from the north of Ireland to the port of Charleston in south Carolina and the Carolina Piedmont, along the Great Wagon Road from Pennsylvania, through the Shenandoah Valley of Virginia, into the western highlands of North Carolina and down to the historic Waxhaws, where President Andrew Jackson spent his childhood and early youth.

On this trail of the Scots-Irish in the Carolinas, five American Presidents emerge as direct descendants of the first frontier Carolina settlers. Also John C. Coulhoun, American Vice-President over two terms, who was the son of an Ulsterman who settled in the Carolina up-country and literally hauled himself up by his bootlaces from a log cabin life to a position as one of the nation's most influential policy makers.

The culture, political heritage and legacy of the Scots-Irish so richly adorn the historical fabric of American life and, through these literary works, people on both sides of the Atlantic can develop an awareness of their illustrious past which will assist them in facing the future with renewed insight and wisdom. These contributions of the Scots-Irish to the building of the great American nation were profound and deserve our full recognition.

Available in hardback and softback from authorised booksellers in the
United Kingdom, the United States and the Republic of Ireland
or direct from the publisher:

Causeway Press & Ambassador Productions Ltd.,
Providence House
16 Hillview Avenue,
Belfast, BT5 6JR

Emerald House Group Inc.
1 Chick Springs Road, Suite 203,
Greenville, South Carolina, 29609

Colloquial Scots-Irish terminology

- *airish* (windy, chilly)
- *backset* (a setback or reversal [in health])
- *beal, bealing* (an abscess, boil, festering sore)
- *bonny-clabber* (curdled sour milk)
- *bottom [s], bottom land* (fertile, low-lying land along a river or creek)
- *chancy* (doubtful, dangerous)
- *contrary* [as a verb] (to vex, oppose)
- *creel* (to twist, wrench, give way)
- *discomfit* (to inconvenience)
- *fireboard* (mantelpiece)
- *hull* (to shell [beans])
- *ill* (bad-tempered)
- *kindling* (twigs, pine needles and scraps of wood to start a fire)
- *let on* (to pretend)
- *mend* (to improve physically)
- *muley* (hornless cow)
- *nicker* (whinny)
- *palings* (pickets of a fence)
- *piece* (distance)
- *redd up* (to tidy up, get a place ready)
- *soon* (early)
- *swan/swanny* (to swear)
- *take up* (begin)

Courtesy of Professor Michael Montgomery, University of South Carolina.